WALKING IN CUMBRIA'S EDEN VALLEY

WALKING IN CUMBRIA'S EDEN VALLEY

30 WALKS BETWEEN THE YORKSHIRE DALES AND THE SOLWAY SALT MARSHES

by Vivienne Crow

CICERONE

JUNIPER HOUSE, MURLEY MOSS,
OXENHOLME ROAD, KENDAL, CUMBRIA LA9 7RL
www.cicerone.co.uk

© Vivienne Crow 2018
Second edition 2018
ISBN: 978 1 85284 901 6
Reprinted 2021 (with updates)
First edition 2011

Printed in Czechia on behalf of Latitude Press Limited on responsibly sourced paper
A catalogue record for this book is available from the British Library.
All photographs are by the author unless otherwise stated.

© Crown copyright 2018 OS PU100012932

Acknowledgements

Charlie Emmett's book *The Eden Way* and John Wyatt's *Cumbria* proved invaluable while researching this guide; and Val Corbett's work, particularly her beautiful photographic collection *A Year in the Life of the Eden Valley*, was a constant source of inspiration.

The author also wishes to thank the following: Mark Hodgkiss and Sandra Pattinson at Cumbria County Council; the ever-friendly and helpful assistants in the Eden Valley tourist information centres; the team at Cicerone, always efficient, knowledgeable and ready to answer even my silliest of queries; the former team at the now defunct East Cumbria Countryside Project for all their hard work paving the way, so to speak, in the Eden Valley, in particular David Nightingale, Dick Capel and Marilyn Leech, for all their encouragement when I worked with them on the Discover Eden Project; David Singleton and Richard Morris, of the Friends of the Settle–Carlisle Line; readers who informed me of changes to routes in the first edition of this book, including Peter Perry and Dave Craggs; and, most of all, Heleyne, for her seemingly infinite patience.

Front cover: Enjoying far-reaching views on the way up to Nine Standards (Walk 3)

CONTENTS

INTRODUCTION 9
The Eden Valley 9
Geology 10
Wildlife and habitats 12
History 14
Weather 18
Where to stay 20
Getting around 21
Waymarking and access 22
Dogs 23
Maps 23
Clothing, equipment and safety 24
Using this guide 25

WALKS 27
Walk 1   Wild Boar Fell 28
Walk 2   Mallerstang Edge and High Seat 34
Walk 3   Nine Standards 39
Walk 4   Smardale Fell and Ash Fell Edge 44
Walk 5   Crosby Garrett Fell and Smardale Gill 48
Walk 6   The Infant Eden and Pendragon Castle 53
Walk 7   Kirkby Stephen to Appleby 59
Walk 8   Great Asby Scar 67
Walk 9   Potts Valley and the Orton Fells 72
Walk 10   Crosby Ravensworth Fell 78
Walk 11   Knipescar Common and River Lowther 83
Walk 12   River Lyvennet at King's Meaburn 88
Walk 13   Rutter Force and Hoff Beck 92
Walk 14   High Cup and Scordale 97
Walk 15   Murton Pike 104
Walk 16   Flakebridge Wood and Dufton Ghyll 107
Walk 17   Dufton Pike 112
Walk 18   High Cup via Great Rundale 116
Walk 19   Cross Fell 120
Walk 20   Long Meg and Her Daughters 125
Walk 21   Melmerby Fell 129
Walk 22   Kirkoswald and Raven Beck 134

Walking in Cumbria's Eden Valley

Walk 23	Armathwaite and Coombs Wood	139
Walk 24	Croglin and Newbiggin	142
Walk 25	Wetheral	146
Walk 26	Talkin Fell and Simmerson Hill	151
Walk 27	Talkin Tarn and the Gelt	155
Walk 28	Quarry Beck and Ridgewood	161
Walk 29	Burgh Marsh	165
Walk 30	Campfield Marsh and Bowness Common	171
Appendix A	Route summary table	176
Appendix B	Useful contacts	178

Updates to this Guide

While every effort is made by our authors to ensure the accuracy of guidebooks as they go to print, changes can occur during the lifetime of an edition. Any updates that we know of for this guide will be on the Cicerone website (www.cicerone.co.uk/901/updates), so please check before planning your trip. We also advise that you check information about such things as transport, accommodation and shops locally. Even rights of way can be altered over time. We are always grateful for information about any discrepancies between a guidebook and the facts on the ground, sent by email to updates@cicerone.co.uk or by post to Cicerone, Juniper House, Murley Moss, Oxenholme Road, Kendal, LA9 7RL.

Register your book: To sign up to receive free updates, special offers and GPX files where available, register your book at www.cicerone.co.uk.

A good track leads back into the valley at the end of Walk 2

Walking in Cumbria's Eden Valley

In woodland beside the River Eden (Walk 7)

INTRODUCTION

On the Pennine Way, looking back towards the Lake District (Walk 14)

THE EDEN VALLEY

If Cumbria's beautiful Eden Valley were anywhere but right next to the Lake District, it would be full of tourists. In reality, few venture this far from Cumbria's best-known National Park, leaving locals to delight in the fact that they have this wonderful area – with its rich natural and human heritage, and its beautiful and diverse landscapes – all to themselves.

From its source high up on the wild moorlands of the North Pennines, incorporated in 2016 into the Yorkshire Dales National Park, to the open spaces of the immense Solway marshes on the Scottish border, the River Eden meanders its way north for 75 wonderful miles. In terms of human history, geology, habitats, wildlife and landscape, walkers couldn't wish for more variety within such a compact area. From Bronze Age settlements, Roman forts and Celtic kingdoms to ruined castles, fortified churches and memories of Bonnie Prince Charlie – the Eden Valley has it all. The landscape alters with every twist and turn of the river – limestone pavement, peaty moorlands and the dramatic Whin Sill of High Cup of the uplands beside the rolling pastures, red sandstone gorges and vast salt marshes in the valley. And walkers are never short of company – from the elusive black grouse, endangered red squirrels and shy otters to huge flocks of noisy waders.

Straddling the river, although not strictly within the area locals refer to as the 'Eden Valley', the largest settlement is the great border city of Carlisle, with its fascinating and often bloody history, changing from English control to Scottish and back again countless times. The attractive market towns of Kirkby Stephen, Appleby-in-Westmorland, Penrith and Brampton also have tonnes of character and are well worth visiting in their own right. They are built mostly from the red sandstone that gives this area such a distinctive look – as are the villages, hamlets, isolated farmhouses and fortified homes that dot the valley and creep up to the very base of the Pennines.

And then there are those views! Wherever you walk in the Eden Valley, the Pennines, particularly Cross Fell, dominate the scenery, and you can also see across to the eastern edge of the Lake District, with Kidsty Pike and Blencathra often standing out on the horizon. As you make your way further downstream, towards the Solway Firth, the Scottish hills begin to appear in the distance: just a dreamy blue outline at first, but then with individual tops becoming more easily identifiable as you head further north.

As well as covering the valley of the River Eden itself, this book includes walks in the dales carved by some of its main tributaries,

Raven Beck (Walk 22)

including the River Lowther, which runs just within the boundaries of the Lake District National Park, the River Lyvennet and the lovely Gelt. And let's not forget the smaller streams too, sometimes just as dramatic and beautiful as their larger siblings – such as Scandal Beck, Hoff Beck, Quarry Beck, Raven Beck and many more. There is also one route (Walk 8) that just falls within the neighbouring catchment of the River Lune.

GEOLOGY

The geology of the Eden Valley is complex, and the experts inevitably interpret it in several different ways. In simple terms, the underlying rock type changes as you move down the

GEOLOGY

hillsides and closer to the river itself, and there are changes too as the river heads downstream.

The River Eden begins its life on the watershed of the high boggy moorlands of the North Pennines. The bedrock here, as in most of the North Pennines and the eastern Lake District fells, is of ancient Ordovician types, laid down by sedimentary processes more than 450 million years ago. These would have started life as a mush of black mud on the sea bed that was then hardened and compressed as the North American and European tectonic plates converged.

The young river, dropping through Hell Gill, quickly leaves the high ground and swings north to enter the narrow glacial valley of Mallerstang. The most noticeable rock type here is carboniferous limestone, capped by broken millstone grit escarpments.

Limestone is an important feature of the Upper Eden Valley, with many tributaries starting life on the pretty grasslands that are characteristic of this rock type. About 350 million years ago, this area would have been covered by a tropical sea that was teeming with life. As generation after generation of these marine invertebrates died, their shells formed a thick layer of sediment on the seabed. This became the pale grey limestone that can be seen just breaking the surface along Lady Anne's Way in Mallerstang or, more obviously, forming large areas of Karst scenery including limestone pavement on Great Asby Scar.

Limestone pavement is the result of the interplay of the soluble nature of the rock and the work of glaciers. About 2.6 million years ago the Earth began to cool, resulting in the formation of glaciers that covered huge

Limestone pavement on Great Asby Scar (Walk 8)

areas of land with massive ice sheets. Although this tends to be called the 'Ice Age', within this Ice Age there were cold periods (glacials) and warmer periods (interglacials) when forests thrived. There were many of these temperature fluctuations, but it is the last cold period, which ended about 10,000 years ago, that has had the most profound effect on the Cumbrian landscape we see today.

The creation of limestone pavement began as the glaciers scoured the rock and ice and fractured it along existing horizontal lines of weakness known as bedding planes. Over time, water has been exploiting the bedding planes and other cracks in the limestone, slowly eroding and dissolving the rock. This has created the fascinating pattern of blocks (clints) and fissures (grikes) that we see today.

One of the most noticeable characteristics of the area closer to the River Eden itself, particularly in its middle reaches, is the new red sandstone. Churches, castles, farms and villages are all built from this distinctive rock, which positively glows as the sun dips towards the horizon at the end of a long summer evening. It does not require a huge leap of the imagination to envisage the desert conditions that created these rocks between the Permian period (280 million years ago) and the beginning of the Triassic (240 million years ago). At this time, what we now call Britain was lying just north of the Equator. Brockram, a breccia visible in the bed of the Eden near Kirkby Stephen, is the oldest of these desert rocks; the new red sandstone is slightly younger.

Hot arid conditions continued into the early part of the Triassic period, but by now seasonal rivers and shallow seas existed too, leaving mudstone deposits known today as the Eden shales. Later still in the Triassic, about 200 million years ago, the Mercia mudstones were deposited. These impervious rocks are found in the lower stretches of the river, near Carlisle.

WILDLIFE AND HABITATS

The plants, animals and birds that thrive in the Eden Valley are as varied as the area's geology and its resulting landscapes. Of course, here, as in all parts of the UK, human beings have had a profound influence, but that is not to say that walkers won't have some fascinating, sometimes even rare, company as they enjoy the routes in this book.

The North Pennines, seemingly bleak and barren at first glance, contain some very important ecosystems. Almost 30 per cent of England's blanket bog is found here, home to peat-building sphagnum moss as well as heather, bog asphodel, crowberry and cotton grass. Rare Alpine plants, such as cloudberry, still thrive on the highest moors.

This locale, designated an Area of Outstanding Natural Beauty, also contains 40 per cent of the UK's

WILDLIFE AND HABITATS

remaining 1100 hectares of upland hay meadows, which burst into life every spring and summer. An amazing tapestry of wildflowers blooms, filling the landscape with vivid colour, from the white of the early flowering wood anemone in March right up until October, when the purple of devil's bit scabious is having its final fling. There can be more than 30 different species growing in every square metre of hay meadow, and up to 100 in any one field, providing a habitat for insects, birds and small mammals such as the increasingly rare water vole.

The moorlands and hay meadows are important for a variety of bird species including red grouse, some of England's last remaining populations of the elusive black grouse, the heavily persecuted and extremely rare hen harrier, the merlin, short-eared owl, skylark, lapwing, golden plover, dunlin, twite, whinchat and wheatear. In spring and early summer the long bubbling song of the curlew may be heard. Having spent the winter on the coast, they and other wading birds move inland in the spring to breed. They particularly favour the rough, rushy allotments above the valley floor and the long grass of the meadows for nesting.

As far as mammals go, the most common species you are likely to see on the uplands is sheep, but there is wildlife too; foxes, hares and stoats can be seen, particularly around dusk and dawn, and further west in the eastern Lake District herds of red deer roam above the tree line. The valleys and low-lying woods are home to badgers, roe deer, voles, shrews, the occasional otter and, of

Wildflower meadow

Walking in Cumbria's Eden Valley

course, red squirrels, sadly threatened by the encroachment of greys into this, one of their last bastions in England. Herons, kingfishers and dippers can often be spotted along the becks and rivers, and the woods are home to wagtails, long-tailed tits, great spotted woodpeckers, cuckoos, siskins, redpolls, finches and warblers among others. Buzzards are probably the most common of the raptors, but small numbers of ospreys, peregrine falcons and, increasingly, red kites can sometimes also be seen.

The limestone grasslands are a delight for amateur botanists. Hoary rock-rose, lily-of-the-valley and many rare orchids can be found on the limestone pavement. In the early summer these areas are full of colour, not only thanks to the vast array of flora but also because of the butterflies that breed here: brimstones, dark green fritillaries, graylings and common blues along with some of England's rarest species such as the Scotch argus.

Having risen in the Yorkshire Dales National Park and skirted the edge of the North Pennines Area of Outstanding Natural Beauty, the River Eden ends its journey at the Solway Coast Area of Outstanding Natural Beauty, another ecologically important locale. This low-lying area includes a wide range of fragile ecosystems, including raised mires, sand dunes, mudflats and salt-marshes. Where the waters of the Eden slowly turn brackish, wildflowers such as marsh samphire (or glasswort),

pennywort and sea thrift thrive. Every winter the entire population of barnacle geese from the Svalbard archipelago in the Arctic Ocean descends on the English and Scottish marshes of the Solway Firth: tens of thousands of birds, impressive both to see and hear. Thousands of other swans, ducks and geese also take advantage of the relatively mild Solway winters, as do snow bunting, twite and glaucous and Iceland gulls. The Solway is also a major migration route for seabirds such as the pomarine skua in the spring and shearwaters and storm petrels in late summer.

Walkers should be aware that, as in most of the UK, there's always a chance of stumbling across adders, our only venomous snake. They're most likely to be spotted on warm days, basking out in the open – sometimes on tracks and paths. Don't be too alarmed, though; the adder will usually make itself scarce as soon as it senses your approach. They bite only as a last resort: if you tread on one or try to pick one up. Even then, for most people, the worst symptoms of an adder bite are likely to be nausea and severe bruising, although medical advice should be sought immediately. It's a different story for our canine friends though: an adder bite can kill dogs.

HISTORY

The River Eden flows through the old counties of Westmorland and Cumberland, which, during the 1974

HISTORY

local government reorganisation, were brought together and combined with parts of Lancashire and Yorkshire to form the modern county of Cumbria. But that does not mean the 'new' county was simply dreamt up by 20th-century bureaucrats; the word 'Cumbria' has its origins in the Celtic words *Cymri* or *Cumber*, meaning 'brothers' or 'countrymen', and the borders of modern-day Cumbria roughly equate to those of the Celtic kingdom of Rheged.

It is thought that people probably first made an appearance in what is today called Cumbria towards the end of the last Ice Age, but these Palaeolithic hunters did not venture very far north. There is evidence, too, of Mesolithic people, but it was really only in Neolithic times that humans began to make their mark on the region. Up until then Mother Nature had been in charge of sculpting the landscape and clothing it as she saw fit, but the late Stone Age heralded a massive revolution as humans began to settle and farm. Neolithic people created clearings in the forests to build their settlements and grow crops, and they used the forests as a wood and timber resource and as grazing and browsing for their livestock.

The arrival of the 'Beaker' people in the Eden Valley early in the second millennium BC heralded the start of the Bronze Age. This period is associated with some of the most enigmatic of prehistoric remains: stone circles such as Long Meg and Mayburgh Henge near Penrith. The next group of 'off-comers' to arrive were the Celts

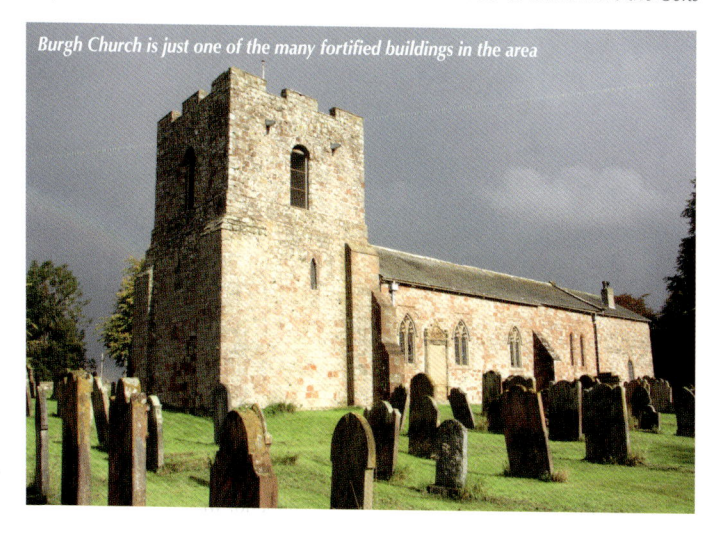

Burgh Church is just one of the many fortified buildings in the area

in about 300BC. These Iron Age people were more sophisticated; they introduced advanced mixed farming techniques to the region as well as their language – a predecessor of modern Welsh. Many of the names of the county's topographical features are Celtic in origin; for example, *blain*, meaning summit, gives rise to 'blen' as in Blencarn.

The Romans arrived in Britain in AD43 and at first the Celts co-operated with the new rulers, living autonomously in their northern kingdom. However, when the Celtic tribes began fighting among themselves the Romans became increasingly involved in the affairs of this remote corner of the empire. But the invaders clearly never saw it as a good place in which to live; it was purely a military zone, and as such there are no villas or markets or even Roman place names, just roads, forts and other defensive structures.

The conquerors finally left this far northwestern outpost to itself in AD410. So began the Dark Ages, a period when fact and fiction became intertwined and semi-mythological figures such as King Arthur and Urien of Rheged appeared. The armies of the north were commanded by Cole Hen, who became king following the Romans' departure – probably the 'Old King Cole' of the nursery rhyme. On his death, his huge kingdom was carved up by his descendants. One of these was Urien, who ruled sixth-century Rheged from his supposed base near modern-day Crosby Ravensworth.

The power of the Celts began to decline in the early seventh century and before long the Anglo-Saxons were the dominant force in much of lowland Cumbria. Their influence can be seen in place names such as Clifton (meaning farmstead on the hill) and in the intricately carved crosses such as the one at St Michael and All Angels Church, Addingham. The uplands, meanwhile, were being settled by pastoralist Vikings who had come from Norway via Ireland and the Isle of Man. Like the Anglo-Saxons, they too left their carved stone emblems, including the Loki Stone in the church at Kirkby Stephen, and remnants of their language. Look at a modern map of Norway and you will quickly discover why the Cumbrians call their hills and mountains fells – *fjell* means 'mountain' in Norwegian. The Norse word for waterfall is *foss*, which becomes 'force' in the Eden Valley, *tjorn* becomes 'tarn', *dalr* becomes 'dale' and *bekkr* 'beck'.

The Normans' Harrying of the North in 1069–70 resulted in a high death toll and the destruction of much of the region's cultivable land, but it wasn't until 1092, when William Rufus decided to build a castle at Carlisle, that the invaders began to take an interest in more direct control of the population. The son of William the Conqueror, William Rufus brought in English settlers who owed their allegiance to the Normans, and he

HISTORY

divided the region up among his barons, who built several castles in the Eden Valley.

Throughout the 12th century and the early part of the 13th century, the stronghold of Carlisle passed from Scottish to English hands and back again several times. It was not until 1216 that the English finally gained control and, except for a brief interlude when Bonnie Prince Charlie captured the city in 1745, it has remained in English hands ever since. But that is not to say that these border regions were forever peaceful after 1216. In fact, Edward I's determination to impose English sovereignty on Scotland marked a resurgence in border difficulties, which continued long after his death at Burgh by Sands in 1307. In the early part of the 14th century, Scottish raiders, led by Robert the Bruce, ransacked much of the north of the county and the villages of the Eden Valley. Towns were burned, churches destroyed and villagers slaughtered. It was a truly grim century for the area, which also had to cope with famines and the Black Death. And, as if all that wasn't enough, the period from the 13th century to the middle of the 17th was also the time of the Border Reivers – the clans that regularly carried out cross-border raids, looting and pillaging and bringing new, bleak words to the English language such as 'bereaved' and 'blackmail'. The fear and insecurity engendered by these bloody times is reflected in the buildings of the era. Churches, such as the one at Burgh by Sands, were fortified, and wealthy families built themselves stout, sturdy refuges, known as pele towers, next to their homes.

Cumberland and Westmorland were slow to pick up on the changes that swept the rest of England during

Drystone walls are a significant feature of the countryside

Walking in Cumbria's Eden Valley

the Agricultural Revolution, partly because of their isolation and partly because the hilly landscape made their circumstances very different from those in the arable south. Drystone walls, still a very important feature of the Eden Valley today, first started appearing from about 1750. Snaking up and down even the steepest of fellsides, these 'enclosures' were stimulated partly by rising food prices, which encouraged farmers to reclaim wasteland and commons. Of course, the region did eventually catch up, and agriculture is now a crucial element of the modern local economy.

If the region was a little slow to join the Agricultural Revolution, it was one of the first in line when it came to the Industrial Revolution. In the North Pennines, lead mining was providing employment for hundreds of people, and the area's wealth of water, in the form of fast-flowing rivers and becks, allowed it to play a significant role in the textile industry, either by providing bobbins for the huge mills of Lancashire and Yorkshire or, in the case of the Carlisle area, by joining the big boys in the making of cloth.

The coming of the railways was one of the main catalysts for industrial development on such a massive scale. Cumbria's first public railway, connecting Carlisle with Newcastle, was completed in 1838, but it was in the 1840s that what we know today as the West Coast Main Line first sliced through the Lune Gorge, up and over the 914ft Shap Summit and on to Carlisle. Then, in 1876, came the Settle–Carlisle Railway, England's last navvy-built line.

WEATHER

There's no denying that Cumbria is a wet county – the Lake District holds the UK record for the highest rainfall in a 24-hour period – but that really is only a tiny fraction of the overall picture. The mountains of the Lake District protect the Eden Valley from the worst of the prevailing south-westerly airflows that bring the wind and rain, so it's slightly drier than much of the county. Even when it does rain, the cloud does not normally hang around for long. If you spend a week in the Eden Valley, you would be unlucky if you had more than one day of constant rainfall; more likely, you will get a few days of sunshine and showers and one or two days of brilliant blue skies. And that applies whatever the time of year. Of course there are some months that tend to be drier than others; early spring and late autumn often hold some pleasant surprises, but don't expect August to be drier than November; it just doesn't work like that in Cumbria.

The wonderful thing about the climate here is that the sky and the quality of the light are ever-changing. You can stand on Cross Fell, the roof of the Pennines, and see curtains of showers coming in from the west, look to the north and the Scottish hills

Winter vista: The River Lowther runs close to the Lake District fells (Walk 11)

will be bathed in sunshine under a cloudless sky, turn round and there are bruised purple storm clouds gathering over County Durham and Northumberland. It's never boring!

As far as temperatures go, Cumbria tends to be cooler than the south of England, but the warming effect of the North Atlantic Drift keeps the mercury above the levels experienced on the eastern side of the Pennines. It also receives regular snowfall, particularly in January and February. This tends to be confined to the higher fells, but the Pennine roads and more isolated valley routes can often become blocked. Cross Fell is often the first county top to receive a dusting of snow, sometimes as early as mid October, and it is also the last to lose its white covering, which can linger well into May.

The weather may not be a crucial factor when doing the low-level walks in this book, but it is an important consideration if you are intending to head on to the open moors. Make sure you get an accurate, mountain-specific weather forecast before setting out. The Lake District forecast provided by the Mountain Weather Information Service (www.mwis.org.uk) covers the whole of Cumbria and the western Pennines north of Ingleborough.

The Helm Wind

The North Pennines and Eden Valley are home to Britain's only named wind. Not unlike the famous *föhn* wind of the Alps, the howling helm wind occurs when a northeasterly airflow hits the Pennine escarpment near Cross Fell. The air climbs the eastern slopes and then comes hurtling down

WALKING IN CUMBRIA'S EDEN VALLEY

the western side at full pelt, meeting the warmer air from the west as it does so. The result is a ferocious easterly wind that lasts for days and can be felt all the way from Brough to Brampton. A visible sign of the wind is the bank of cloud that forms just above the fell-tops, sometimes covering Cross Fell. This is known as the 'helm cloud' or simply the 'helm'. Another bank of cloud, known as the 'helm bar' sometimes forms parallel to the helm cloud.

A particularly strange, slightly disturbing aspect of the helm is the way that just a few miles to the west of the fellside settlements the wind simply dies. You can stand in Penrith without a hint of a breeze and listen to the roar of the helm wind to the east.

WHERE TO STAY

There is a good range of both self-catering and bed and breakfast accommodation throughout the Eden Valley. Most towns and villages have a number of guesthouses, hotels and inns, and there are also plenty of more isolated farmhouse B&Bs scattered throughout the area. Prices tend to be slightly lower than in the neighbouring Lake District, but the quality is often just as high. Visitor numbers are higher during the school holidays, but you are unlikely to experience any problems finding somewhere to stay, although Appleby becomes rather busy during the horse fair at the beginning of June each year.

For budget travellers, there are hostels at Kirkby Stephen and Dufton, the former a stopping-off point for walkers doing Wainwright's Coast to Coast walk, and the latter especially popular with backpackers on the Pennine Way. If you are looking for somewhere to pitch your tent, then www.ukcampsite.co.uk is a good place to start your search.

Kirkby Stephen and Appleby are probably the best bases for the walks in this book, particularly if you're relying on public transport, but Crosby Ravensworth, Ravenstonedale, Dufton, Kirkoswald, Wetheral and Brampton are also very pleasant and interesting places to stay. If you're having a break from the walking, there are castles, ruined abbeys, picturesque churches, gardens and nature reserves to visit. The border city of Carlisle is well worth a trip in its own right; the medieval castle and beautiful cathedral both have fascinating histories, and the award-winning Tullie House Museum and Art Gallery contains lots of cleverly designed exhibits that tell the fascinating story of the city in an interesting and accessible way.

The local tourist information centres, listed in Appendix B, are a good place to start your search for accommodation. The staff are normally both friendly and knowledgeable. Cumbria Tourism's website also contains a wide selection of properties: www.golakes.co.uk. Don't be put off by the name; it covers the whole of Cumbria.

The attractive market town of Appleby

GETTING AROUND

The Eden Valley and nearby towns are surprisingly well served in terms of the national rail network. The West Coast Main Line, linking London Euston with Glasgow, passes through east Cumbria. All trains stop at Carlisle, and some also stop at Penrith North Lakes. With large stretches of the line capable of handling trains travelling at speeds of up to 125mph, it is now possible to travel the 310 miles from London to Carlisle in as little as 3hr 15min. The journey time from Glasgow to Carlisle is about 1hr 7min.

Carlisle, Wetheral and Brampton are on the line to Newcastle with trains roughly every hour. The journey time from Newcastle to Carlisle is about 1hr 25min. There are also about seven trains a day from Leeds to Carlisle (journey time 2hr 45min). This journey is made via the scenic Settle–Carlisle railway, famously saved from the axe in the 1980s. Trains on this line also stop at various points throughout the Eden Valley, including Armathwaite, Lazonby, Langwathby, Appleby-in-Westmorland, Kirkby Stephen and, just outside the area, remote Garsdale. Inevitably, it is a popular line with walkers, and two linear routes in this guide make use of it (Walk 1 and Walk 7).

National Express runs several daily services from London to Carlisle (journey times roughly 7–9hr). There are also a few coaches every day linking Carlisle with Glasgow (journey time 2hr), Manchester (3hr 15min) and Birmingham International Airport (5hr). National Express also has a daily service between Inverness

Waymarking tends to be good on the walks

and London Victoria that stops in Penrith (journey time to London 6hr 30min).

Outside the main towns, the area is poorly served by local buses. Looking at a list of services for the area east of the Eden, there may appear to be lots of buses, but look again and you'll see most of these operate just once a week, twice if you're lucky. They're of little practical use to walkers and so are not listed in the 'transport' section for each walk.

For information on bus and rail routes and timetables, phone Traveline on 0871 200 2233 or visit the website: www.traveline.info.

WAYMARKING AND ACCESS

Most of the walks in this guide make use of the Eden Valley's superb network of public rights of way. Although some of the paths and bridleways are surprisingly little used, particularly across farmland and through pleasant riverside meadows, they are still reasonably well signposted and a succession of gates and stiles guide the way. Walkers have the former East Cumbria Countryside Project to thank for much of the work that was done on waymarking, installing path furniture and opening up new routes. Sadly, the organisation no longer exists, a victim of budget cuts.

A few of the walks also cross areas of open moorland that have been designated 'access land' under the Countryside and Rights of Way Act (CRoW) 2000. This Act gave people the right to walk across land thus designated on maps – mostly mountains, moor, heath and common land – without having to stick to rights of way. Although most areas are open all of the time, restrictions can be imposed to protect wildlife, farm livestock and the public for up to 28 days a year, for example, when grouse shooting is taking place. For more information relating to dogs on access land, see below.

Information on access land restrictions and closures is usually posted at major access points, but you can check in advance on Natural England's 'CRoW and coastal access maps' at www.openaccess.naturalengland.org.uk.

Eden Benchmarks
Walkers will come across some interesting art projects as they wander the paths of the Eden Valley. One of these is the Eden Benchmarks, a series of sculptures commissioned by the East Cumbria Countryside Project to celebrate the new millennium. Each by a different artist, they have been installed at various locations beside public paths along the entire length of the River Eden. Each also functions as a seat. The artists' brief was to produce sculptures that harmonised with the landscape and captured the essence of each locality. The first is *Water Cut* by Mary Bourne, located high on the wild moorland close to the source of the river at Mallerstang. The other nine are at Kirkby Stephen, Temple Sowerby, Appleby, Lazonby, Edenhall, Armathwaite, Wetheral, Bitts Park in Carlisle and Rockcliffe, close to the mouth of the river.

DOGS

Most of the walks in this book follow public rights-of-way from start to finish and, as such, there are no restrictions on dog access. However, where a route crosses access land but is not on a right-of-way, walkers need to check access rights. The landowner has a right to ban dogs, usually for reasons relating to grouse moorland management. Restrictions, which are subject to change, can be found at www.openaccess.naturalengland.org.uk.

Dog owners should always be sensitive to the needs of livestock and wildlife. The law states that dogs have to be controlled so that they do not scare or disturb livestock or wildlife, including ground-nesting birds. On access land, they have to be kept on leads of no more than 2 metres long from 1 March to 31 July – and all year round near sheep. A dog chasing lambing sheep can cause them to abort. Remember that, as a last resort, farmers can shoot dogs to protect their livestock.

Cattle, particularly cows with calves, may very occasionally pose a risk to walkers with dogs. If you ever feel threatened by cattle, let go of your dog's lead and let it run free.

MAPS

The map extracts used in this book are taken from the Ordnance Survey's 1:50,000 Landranger series. They are meant as a guide only and walkers are advised to purchase the relevant

Pausing on the Faraday Gill path (Walk 3)

map(s), and know how to navigate using them, before setting off. The whole area is covered by sheets 85, 86, 90, 91 and 98.

The OS 1:25,000 Explorer series provides greater detail, showing field boundaries as well as the extent of access land. To complete all the walks in this guide using Explorer maps, you will need sheets 315, OL5, OL31 and OL19.

CLOTHING, EQUIPMENT AND SAFETY

The amount of gear you carry with you on a walk and the clothes you choose to wear will differ according to the length of the walk, the time of year and the terrain you are likely to encounter. Preparing for the 22km hike across the exposed moorland above Murton requires considerably more thought than when setting out on a 6km Sunday morning stroll from Armathwaite. As such, this section is aimed at those heading out in the winter or venturing on to the higher ground; summer or valley walkers should adjust their kit accordingly.

Even in the height of summer, your daysack should contain everything you need to make yourself wind- and waterproof. Most people will also carry a few extra layers of clothing; this is more important if you are heading on to higher ground where the weather can be unpredictable and prone to sudden change. As far as footwear goes, some walkers like good, solid leather boots with plenty of ankle support, while others prefer something lighter. Whatever you wear, make sure it has a good grip and is unlikely to result in a twisted ankle on uneven ground. You may also consider investing in gaiters, particularly if you are hoping to walk several of the Pennine routes, where it can be boggy.

Every walker needs to carry a map and compass, and know how to use them. Always carry sufficient food and water to sustain you during the walk and provide extra emergency rations in case you are out for longer than you originally planned. Emergency equipment should include a torch and a whistle, the distress signal being six flashes/whistle-blasts repeated at 1min intervals. Pack a small first aid kit too.

Carry a fully charged mobile phone, just in case of a genuine emergency. If things do go badly wrong and you need help, first make sure you have a note of all the relevant details such as your location, the nature of the injury or problem, the number of people in the party and your mobile phone number. Only then should you dial 999 and ask for the police, then mountain rescue.

Walkers should also remember that, as with anywhere in the country, the waterside paths used in this guidebook might become waterlogged or even flooded after periods of exceptional rain. Parts of Burgh Marsh (Walk 29) may also become inundated at times of particularly high tides.

While mobile phone coverage can be patchy in Mallerstang and some of the Eden Valley's more isolated villages, the signal tends to be good on higher ground.

USING THIS GUIDE

The routes in this book are designed to give the walker a taste of everything the Eden Valley has to offer. From peaceful woodland strolls to serious moorland hikes, and from explorations of the limestone uplands to walks on the Solway marshes, they visit just about every nook and cranny of this beautiful area.

Since the first edition of *Walking in Cumbria's Eden Valley* was published in 2011, parts of the area have been incorporated into the Yorkshire Dales National Park. This new edition reflects that change and includes several more walks in what has become known as the 'Westmorland Dales'.

The walks also take in many of the river's tributaries, just straying on one occasion into the Lake District National Park. However, Ullswater, Patterdale and the parts of the Northern Fells that also fall into the Eden catchment have been deliberately missed out because they're already covered by scores of walking guides to the Lake District.

The walks are ordered from source to sea, starting from the head of the river in the south and gradually working their way north to where the Eden meets the Solway Firth. Most of the routes are circular, but there are two linear walks that make use of the Settle–Carlisle railway (Walk 1 and Walk 7). Check timetables carefully to make sure you have enough time to complete the route.

Looking out over the Eden Valley from Lazonby

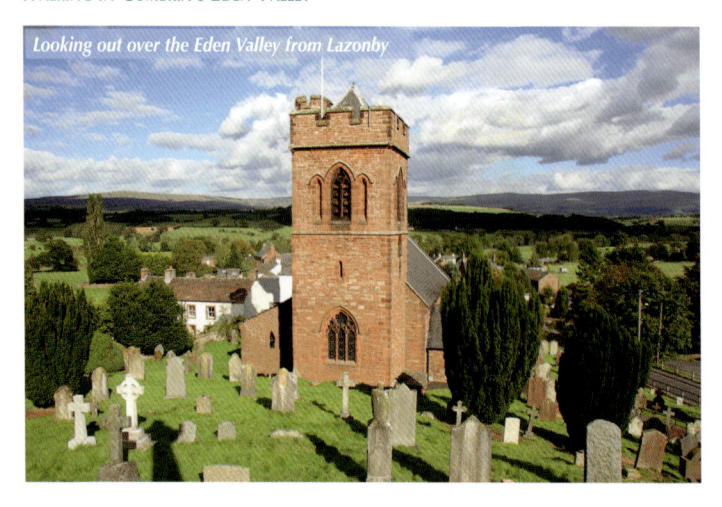

GPX tracks

GPX tracks for the routes in this guidebook are available to download free at www.cicerone.co.uk/901/GPX. A GPS device is an excellent aid to navigation, but you should also carry a map and compass and know how to use them.

Each walk is graded one to five, one being the easiest, but please note that these ratings are subjective, and walkers are advised to read the route description before setting out, to gain a better understanding of what to expect. It may be a good idea to do an easy walk first and then judge the rest accordingly. There is a route summary table at the back of the book in Appendix A to help you find a route quickly that meets your requirements.

WALKING IN CUMBRIA'S EDEN VALLEY

The track heading north from Longdales (Walk 23)

WALKING IN CUMBRIA'S EDEN VALLEY

WALK 1
Wild Boar Fell

Start	Garsdale railway station (SD 788 917)
Finish	Kirkby Stephen railway station (NY 761 067)
Distance	12¼ miles (19.5km)
Total ascent	688m (2257ft)
Grade	5
Time	7hr
Terrain	Field paths; tracks; open moor, boggy in places
Maps	OS Explorer OL19 or OS Landrangers 98 and 91
Transport	The start and finish are both on the Settle–Carlisle railway
Facilities	Variety of pubs and cafés in Kirkby Stephen

Mallerstang is a remote valley on the Cumbria–North Yorkshire border, the point at which the River Eden emerges from its peaty source on Black Fell Moss, plummets down through Hell Gill and begins its long journey north to the Solway Firth. This wonderfully wild day on the hills on the western side of the valley is walked in the company of curlews and golden plover. Ordnance Survey maps show no paths on lonely Swarth Fell (681m/2234ft) and Wild Boar Fell (708m/2322ft), but in reality there are routes on the ground and the walls and fences also aid navigation. Nonetheless, this walk is best saved for a clear day, if only to appreciate the magnificent views of the Howgills, the North Pennines and even the Lake District.

Leave **Garsdale station** and turn right along the minor road down to a T-junction with the **A684**. Cross over and go through a gated stile in the wall opposite. There isn't a clear path on the ground; simply keep about 40m between yourself and the wall on your left, and you will reach a squeeze stile. Go through and continue in roughly the same direction.

Beyond the next gated stile, head north-northwest along the grassy path – in the general direction of Swarth Fell. Go through two kissing-gates in quick succession

WALK 1 – WILD BOAR FELL

THE SETTLE–CARLISLE RAILWAY

The Settle–Carlisle Railway was the last mainline railway in England to be constructed almost entirely by hand. Carving its convoluted route through the Pennines, it was a major feat of engineering and the statistics bear this out. Work on the 72-mile line began in 1869 and lasted for seven years. The line opened to passengers on 1 May 1876 and includes 14 tunnels and more than 20 viaducts. The Ribblehead Viaduct is 400m long and 30.5m above the ground. The longest tunnel, Blea Moor, is 2404m long. About 6000 men were involved in building it. Many workers were injured or killed during the construction, and many more died through outbreaks of smallpox and other diseases which spread quickly in the makeshift, unhygienic settlements in which they lived.

The line has famously survived two attempts to close it: once in the early 1960s and again in the 1980s.

next to the house at **Blake Mire**. Turn right along a rough track for 75m and then bear left along a narrow, grassy path heading northwest. This passes through a gap in a wall about 50m to the left of a small barn. Following the waymarker posts, continue in the same direction to go through a stile. Drop to some ruined buildings, picking up a rough track en route. Follow this to a surfaced lane and turn right. ▶

This pretty spot is known as Grisedale, 'valley of the wild boar'.

Remote Garsdale station

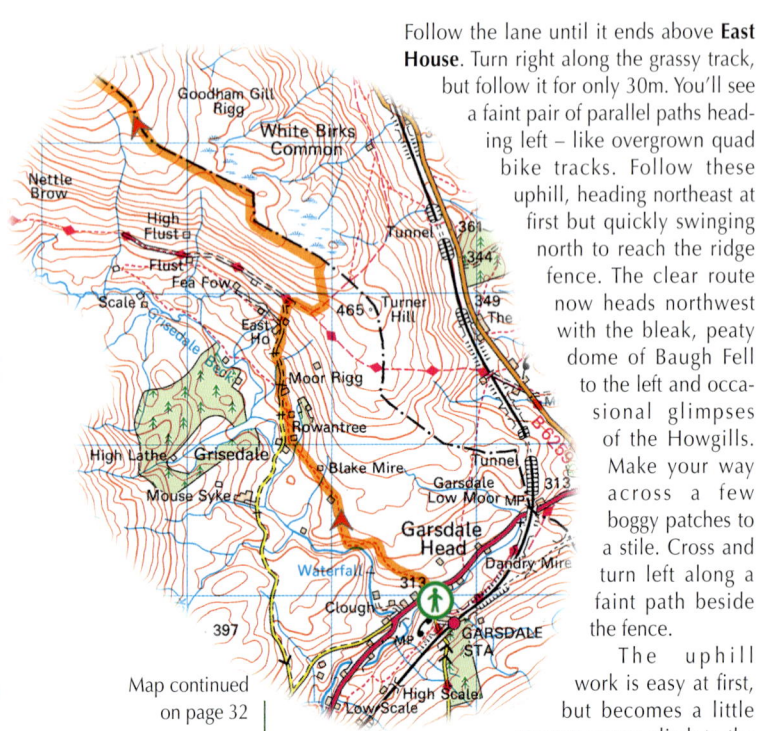

Follow the lane until it ends above **East House**. Turn right along the grassy track, but follow it for only 30m. You'll see a faint pair of parallel paths heading left – like overgrown quad bike tracks. Follow these uphill, heading northeast at first but quickly swinging north to reach the ridge fence. The clear route now heads northwest with the bleak, peaty dome of Baugh Fell to the left and occasional glimpses of the Howgills. Make your way across a few boggy patches to a stile. Cross and turn left along a faint path beside the fence.

Map continued on page 32

You can now see right across the top of the Howgills to the Lake District.

The uphill work is easy at first, but becomes a little steeper as you climb to the cairn on **Swarth Fell Pike**. The path swings away from the fence slightly but continues parallel with it – and then a wall – to reach the highest point on Swarth Fell proper. ◀

Follow the wall into the saddle between Swarth Fell and **Wild Boar Fell**. Here, as you pass a long thin tarn, given the name Swarth Fell Tarn in July 2017, the wall swings left. Continue straight on alongside the fence for the time being. About halfway up the next slope, bear right (northeast) at a fork. Instead of climbing to the trig point, this path hugs the escarpment edge, which it reaches near a line of tall cairns (not marked on the map).

WALK 1 – WILD BOAR FELL

The eastern edge of Wild Boar Fell is marked by a line of tall cairns

As with so many Cumbrian fells, there is a legend behind the name '**Wild Boar**'. England's last wild boar, before the packs now roaming south-west England escaped from captivity, is said to have been killed on Wild Boar Fell by Sir Richard de Musgrave, who lived at Hartley Castle. A boar's tusk was later found in his tomb in Kirkby Stephen parish church.

If you thought the views were good up to this point, you're in for a treat now. Cross the ladder stile and, ignoring the path heading northwest towards the cairn and trig point, keep right to follow a faint path along the edge of the fell. Huge slabs of rock lie in piles at the foot of the crags to your right. More than 400m below, the infant River Eden snakes its way through a magnificent valley at the start of its long journey to the Solway Firth. Further north, the valley widens as the river skirts the base of the highest of the Pennines, including Cross Fell.

Dropping from the summit area, you reach a wall where you cross the route of the Pennine Bridleway. Don't go through the gate; instead, continue in roughly

31

WALKING IN CUMBRIA'S EDEN VALLEY

Map continued on page 33

the same direction, with the wall on your left. When the wall swings left, keep straight ahead (north) on a gently rising path that leads on to **Little Fell**. From the cairn at its northern end, the path continues north across the open, grassy fellside.

You'll pick up the line of another wall – this one on your right. Follow it for about 140m and then bear left at a fork, heading north on to **Greenlaw Rigg**. The path is reasonably clear as it then descends northwest, but becomes less obvious in its final stages. At this point, walk north and you'll quickly reach a minor road. Turn left along the asphalt for 350m. Take the bridleway signposted to the right. Keep straight on at a crossing of paths and you'll soon see two tracks passing under the railway. Keep left to pass through the more northerly of two gaps.

Beyond the railway, drystone walls channel the path down to a farm track, along which you bear left. Drawing level with the end of the last building on your left, bear right to follow a rough track down to a pair of gates. Go through the one on the left and climb to a gate to the right of the picturesque ruins of **Lammerside Castle**.

Lammerside Castle was built in the 12th century and was then strengthened in the 14th century to provide protection against

Scottish raiders. It was occupied by the Wharton family, but they abandoned it in the 17th century when they moved to the nearby fortified manor house, Wharton Hall, which dates from the early 15th century.

Head north into the middle of the field and then drop northeast through a small gate in the field corner. Go through another gate opposite and then continue in the same direction. Once through the next gate, follow the fence on your right until the field narrows. Go through the large metal gate on your left and turn right along the concrete track. Ignore the turning on your right.

As you reach **Wharton Hall**, take the track on the left – heading uphill to the right of a slurry tank. This quickly leads to a gate. Go through and turn right, walking parallel with a wall to the right. Go through a gate in another wall and head downhill, to the left of a large tree. A small gate provides access to a clear track, along which you turn left.

Just before the cattle grid at **Halfpenny House**, turn left along the shared walkway and cycle path. This leads up to **Kirkby Stephen station**'s access lane.

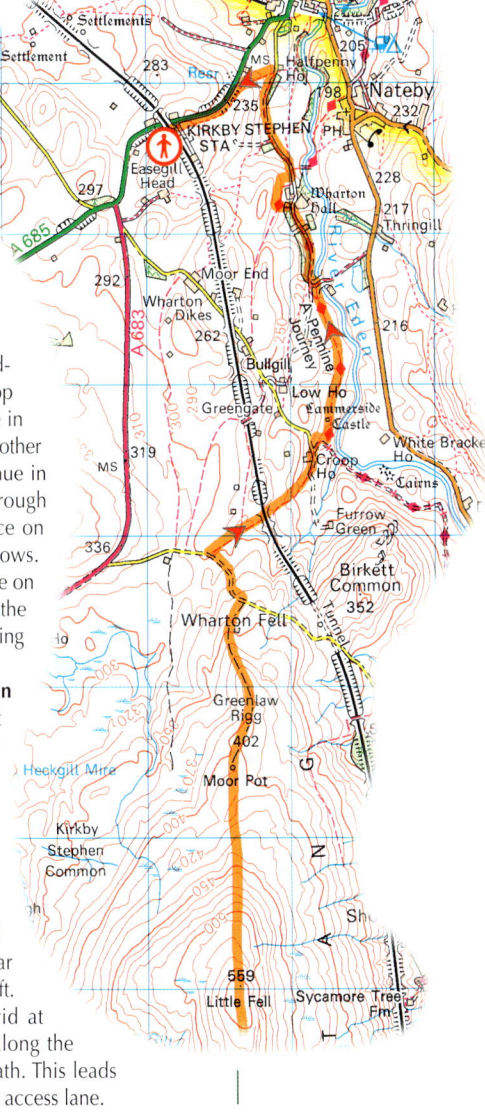

WALK 2

Mallerstang Edge and High Seat

Start/finish	Roadside parking beside Thrang Beck, about 135m south of The Thrang on the B6259 through Mallerstang (NY 783 005)
Distance	10¼ miles (16.5km)
Total ascent	579m (1900ft)
Grade	4
Time	5¾hr
Terrain	Ascent largely pathless; open moorland, boggy in places; good track on return
Maps	OS Explorer OL19 or OS Landranger 98 and 91
Transport	None
Facilities	Nateby Inn in nearby Nateby

This grand day out on the moorland on the eastern side of Mallerstang, reaching a high point of 709m (2325ft) on High Seat, is the stuff of which memories are made. It's not just the open expanses of these high, windswept moors that make it such a special day – it's the off-piste route up through the wild country at the base of Mallerstang Edge; it's the stupendous views from the airy edge of the craggy escarpment; it's the haunting call of the elusive golden plovers on High Pike Hill; and the long, easy descent into a magnificent dale at the end of the outing.

Walk north along the **B6259**. About 450m beyond **Outhgill**, take the footpath signposted through the large metal gate set back from the road on the right. In about 45m, go through a small gate on the left. A faint trail heads uphill through the trees, following the line of a tiny beck at first and then swinging left to cross a stile around the back of the buildings at **Ing Hill**.

Walk with the field boundary on your left and then cross a stile in it. Head roughly north across the pasture and go through a gate between two cottages. Continue to a rough track and turn right – passing through a small gate to the left of a garage. Keep straight on, at first with a beck on your left and then steadily rising between two walls.

The next gate leads on to access land. Cross to the north side of **Castlethwaite Gill** and follow it upstream. Soon after a gate leading into an area of saplings fenced for their protection, swing left with the wall. For the next 320m or so, progress is slow as you tackle some rough, damp ground. After crossing a gill, head up to the right on a tongue of land between the gill you've just crossed and a shallower gully to the left. Leave the fenced area via a wooden gate.

The next section of the walk is totally pathless and there are no walls or fences to guide you. Look to the east and you'll see a ridge dropping northwest towards the head of the beck you recently crossed. Head for the

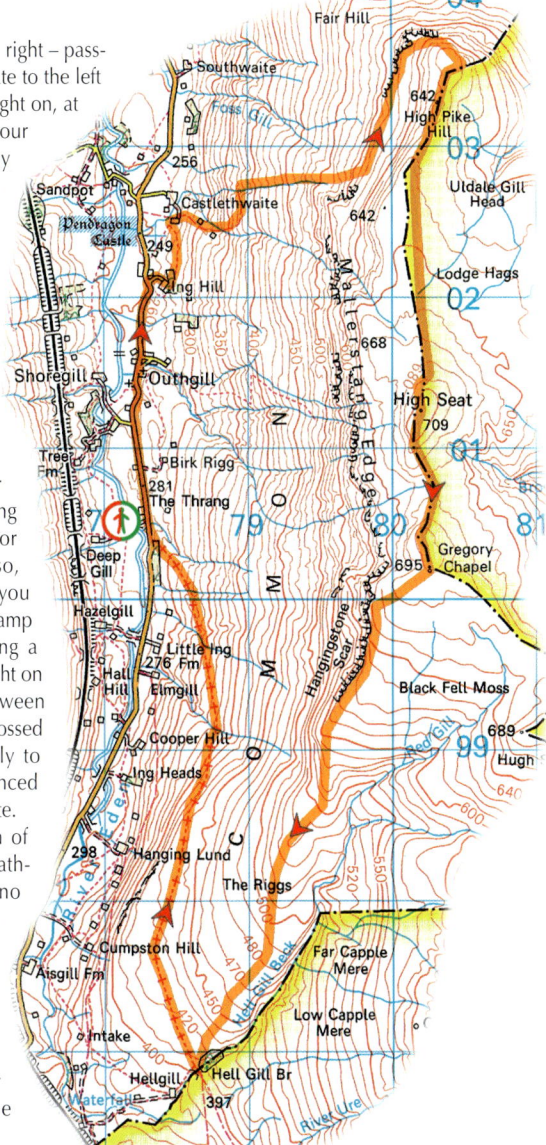

Quarry workings above Mallerstang

slightly gentler ground at the base of this ridge. This is achieved by walking east for 340m and then briefly veering east-northeast. You may be lucky enough to pick up a faint path through the scattered boulders here, but don't rely on it – it's difficult to find and it's intermittent.

As you steadily climb, the landscape becomes more dramatic – rockier and steeper – although our route avoids any tricky ground. You'll pass about 180m to the north of Bleakham Nook, a bowl of shattered rocks lying at the foot of the ridge. Now veer slightly left to ascend through the hummocks of Bleakham Hills.

Eventually, you'll reach easier ground on a broad, grassy shelf just below the main ridge. Stride out northnortheast along this lofty ledge to reach a tall cairn. This marks the edge of a disused quarry. You could now strike off right to climb directly to **High Pike Hill**, but it's more interesting to continue north on the faint trail through the workings. It also gives you time to enjoy the views of the North Pennines straight ahead.

Reaching the northern end of the workings and a smaller cairn, follow the trail round to the right, but then leave it just before it cuts across steeper ground. Head

WALK 2 – MALLERSTANG EDGE AND HIGH SEAT

up to the right here (east-southeast) on grass and mosses, keeping to the right of the steep, rocky ground. As the gradient eases, swing southeast across tussocky, boggy ground to reach the main ridge path.

Turn right, soon reaching the cairn on top of **High Pike Hill**. The next summit is **High Seat**, 2.1km south of here. The path makes a beeline for it. It becomes a little unclear as it crosses a flat, stony area. When it does so, simply continue south.

We've now entered golden plover territory. ▶ As the ground begins rising towards **High Seat**, you reach an area of peat hags. Bear right (southwest) at a fork here to avoid the worst of the boggy ground. The path soon regains its southward trajectory – up the damp but otherwise easy slopes.

The views from the ridge have been rather uninspiring up until now, but things change when you reach the cairn on High Seat (709m/2325ft). As well as being able to look across the Eden Valley to Wild Boar Fell and the Howgills beyond, you can see all of the Yorkshire 'three peaks': Ingleborough and Whernside straight ahead, and, slightly further east, Pen-y-ghent.

At nesting time, the golden plovers' high-pitched, plaintive calls bring a melancholy atmosphere to these vast, empty uplands.

Whernside and Ingleborough from Mallerstang Edge

37

Drop southeast on a broad, grassy path that crosses damp ground at Steddale Mouth. It now climbs west-southwest to climb back on to the high ground. When you reach the pile of stones at Archy Styrigg, also known as **Gregory Chapel**, bear right.

The fairly clear path drops southwest towards the precipitous escarpment edge. The way ahead becomes less obvious where you have to negotiate some damp ground, but you'll quickly pick up a clear path along the top of the sheer crags of **Hangingstone Scar**. This airy promenade provides a fine perspective on **Mallerstang Edge**: its line of shattered cliffs leads north for two miles, as far back as Bleakham Nook, with enormous boulder fields littering the slopes below.

The path slowly drops to a cairn. From here, the descent continues down the dreary slopes of **The Riggs** – enlivened in spring and early summer by the bubbling trill of curlews. The general direction is southwest, although the indistinct path weaves about in a bid to avoid the horrible bogs that lurk nearby. **Hell Gill Beck**, which soon becomes the River Eden, is over to the left.

As a narrow strip of conifers comes into view, aim for its lower end. On reaching a wall, turn right along the track. You're now following the route of several long-distance paths including the Pennine Bridleway, Wainwright's Pennine Journey and Lady Anne's Way.

> **The Lady Anne's Way** is a 160km (100-mile) walk inspired by the routes taken by Lady Anne Clifford from her castle in Skipton to visit the Westmorland estates she fought for in the 17th century. For more on Lady Anne's legacy, see Walk 7.

The track passes across limestone grassland frequented by lapwings to reach Mary Bourne's Water Cut, one of the Eden Benchmark sculptures, and then gradually descends to the valley. When you reach the road, turn right to return to the parking area.

WALK 3
Nine Standards

Start/finish	Large layby at Cumbria's border with North Yorkshire on the B6270 (NY 811 040)
Distance	7 miles (11.5km)
Total ascent	384m (1260ft)
Grade	3
Time	3¾hr
Terrain	Open moorland, boggy in places; section on road
Maps	OS Explorer OL19 or OS Landranger 91
Transport	None
Facilities	Nateby Inn nearby Nateby

Nine Standards Rigg, high above the Upper Eden Valley, is crowned by a group of mysterious 'stone men'. Located close to the 662m (2171ft) summit of the hill, these tall cairns can be seen for miles around. Likewise, the view from this windswept spot is extensive in all directions. Nine Standards is usually climbed from Kirkby Stephen in the valley below, but this walk makes use of a substantial layby located more than 500m above sea level to reduce the amount of climbing. It passes through attractive limestone country before climbing to the summit, where a toposcope provides details of the hills that can be seen. A peaty path, part of Wainwright's popular Coast to Coast route, then heads south across this vast area of moorland.

From the layby on the county border, walk northwest along the **B6270** for about 320m – until you see a sign on the right explaining the various seasonal routes used by Wainwright's Coast to Coast. Take the broad, grassy path heading roughly north – the Coast to Coast's December-to-April option and bad-weather alternative. Bear right when this forks in a short while.

Walking in Cumbria's Eden Valley

The 190-mile **Coast to Coast long-distance walk** was devised by the guidebook writer Alfred Wainwright in 1972. Starting in St Bees in Cumbria and ending in Robin Hood's Bay in North Yorkshire, it crosses three National Parks: the Lake District, the Yorkshire Dales and the North York Moors.

Go through a gate and walk across a fenced area of exposed limestone. After the next gate, bear left to walk beside the fence. Then, at the next gate, swing right on a reasonably clear path crossing **Lamps Moss**.

Near the head of the impressive limestone gorge of Dukerdale, you'll see some huge holes, like bomb craters, beside the path. These are **shake holes**, a common feature of limestone areas. They are formed when rainwater washes the subsurface soil down into cracks in the underlying rock. Eventually the ground collapses, leaving a small depression.

As another path joins from the left, drop to cross the beck feeding into Dukerdale. Climbing the slope on the other side, bear right at a fork. This path gradually swings away from the wall. After crossing Rollinson Gill, it zig-zags up a grassy slope to a small stone

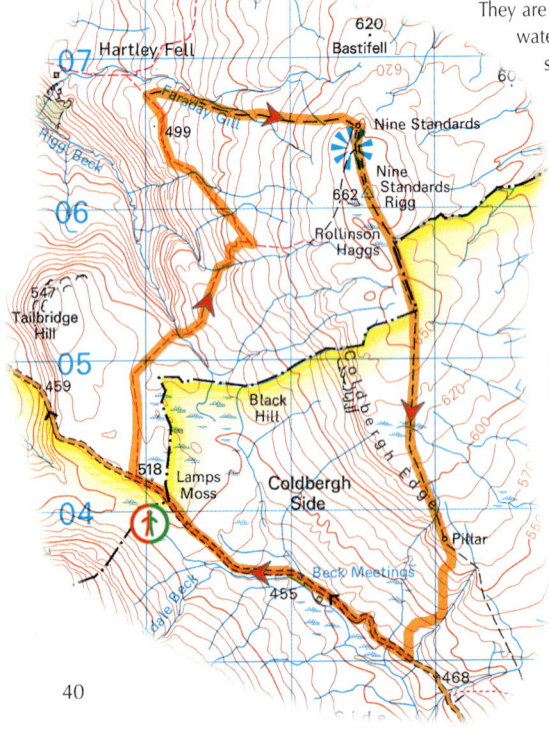

Dukerdale

construction on the high ground. Pass to the left of this and keep straight ahead (east) to reach a fingerpost. Turn left here – along a narrow, grassy path that heads northwest at first.

Pay particularly close attention to the path and the walk description for the next few hundred metres; it's easy to go wrong here, especially if you're distracted by the beautiful views of the Lake District and the North Pennines that are starting to open out.

You'll soon reach a fingerpost beside a tiny beck. It's very tempting here to keep straight on, but you need to bear left, heading downhill. Soon after the next waymarker, as the path becomes less distinct, you encounter a very soggy gill. Bear left here, heading downstream, and you'll quickly hit a clearer path. Turn right, quickly crossing the beck.

This relatively dry, grassy path – with a wall to the left – makes for easy walking. When you reach a fingerpost in a few hundred metres, turn sharp right – signposted Nine Standards.

Nine Standards

Having wound your way uphill for a short while, you'll see **Faraday Gill** to the left: a rocky and steep-sided trench cutting into the grassy moorland. The path leads directly to the **Nine Standards** themselves.

The origin of the '**stone men**' or tall cairns on Nine Standards Rigg is a mystery. One claim is that they were constructed by the Romans to look like troops from a distance; others say they are boundary markers. Major repairs on some of the cairns were carried out in 2005. There is a tremendous view from the top, taking in the Lake District fells, Cross Fell – the highest point in the Pennines – and countless other hills stretching far into the distance.

For a detailed breakdown of exactly what it is you're looking at, head roughly south-southwest for about 90m to reach the toposcope, or view indicator. From here, the faint path continues south-southeast to the trig pillar.

The march of tens of thousands of Coast to Coast walkers' boots have created a path of sorts continuing

WALK 3 – NINE STANDARDS

from the trig pillar. It drops, via a fingerpost, to cross the new flagstones over the boggy ground at Cumbria's border with North Yorkshire. ▶

Another fingerpost marks the point at which the seasonal Coast to Coast routes split. Having started the walk on the green route, we're now following the red route, which keeps straight on. Although it weaves about, the general direction is slightly east of south. The path is little more than a worn line through the moorland vegetation, so it's easy to lose sight of it, particularly where it crosses boggy sections.

About 2.6km beyond Nine Standards, the route passes to the left of a pile of stones near **Coldbergh Edge**. From here, it continues south-southeast towards a tall cairn close to some rock outcrops.

About 90m beyond the cairn, leave the Coast to Coast as it heads left at a faint path fork. Our route takes the more pleasant-looking grassy track that swings right. This later joins up with a more solid track that descends to the road. Turn right. There's now about 2.2km of road-walking back to the layby where the walk started.

Before flagstones were laid, this section of the Coast to Coast was notoriously tricky. Mountain rescue volunteers had even been called out to pull walkers from the bog. The new path was opened in 2017.

Enjoying the view from Coldbergh Edge

Walking in Cumbria's Eden Valley

WALK 4
Smardale Fell and Ash Fell Edge

Start/finish	King's Head pub in Ravenstonedale (NY 721 043)
Distance	7¾ miles (12.5km)
Total ascent	308m (1010ft)
Grade	2–3
Time	3½hr
Terrain	Meadows; low moorland; short section on road
Maps	OS Explorer OL19 or OS Landranger 91
Transport	None
Facilities	King's Head and Black Swan in Ravenstonedale

Smardale Fell and Ash Fell are two areas of relatively low-lying moorland to the southwest of Kirkby Stephen. While Smardale Fell is fairly well visited by walkers, particularly those of the Coast-to-Coast variety, Ash Fell remains off the radars of most people. They don't know what they're missing! Even though it reaches only 385m (1263ft) above sea level, the limestone ridge that forms the southern edge of the fell makes for great walking. Easy underfoot and with superb views, it's an absolute delight to stride out along it and then return to the lovely village of Ravenstonedale via beckside meadows.

With your back to the King's Head, turn right along the lane and then left at the road junction. Immediately after the bridge over **Scandal Beck**, take the track on the right. Just after passing under the **A685**, go through the small gate on the right close to a metal bridge. Don't cross this; instead, bear left to head upstream beside Scandal Beck.

After the next gate, turn right. Beyond another gate in a short while, keep straight ahead and you'll find a pedestrian gate on the other side of the small building. Follow the beck downstream and you'll soon join a track heading in your direction. About 75m after the track swings away from the fence on the right, turn right at a waymarker post and make your way over to a gate.

WALK 4 – SMARDALE FELL AND ASH FELL EDGE

Beyond this, veer left to climb a steep, grassy slope. The path isn't obvious, but two waymarker posts lead the way. The higher of the two indicates a swing to the right. At the top of the slope, head north, aiming for the eastern edge of a small conifer plantation. Smardale Viaduct soon comes into view further down the valley.

Having crossed a stile next to a large metal gate, the route passes to the right of the plantation. After the next gate and stile, head slightly east of north to drop to a gated stile in a wall.

On the other side, turn right along the track. After crossing **Smardale Bridge**, you briefly join the route of the Coast to Coast. Head uphill on a clear path between two walls. After the next gate, the grassy track swings up to the left; one more gate and heather becomes more common. Keep close to the wall as the path eases its way steadily higher.

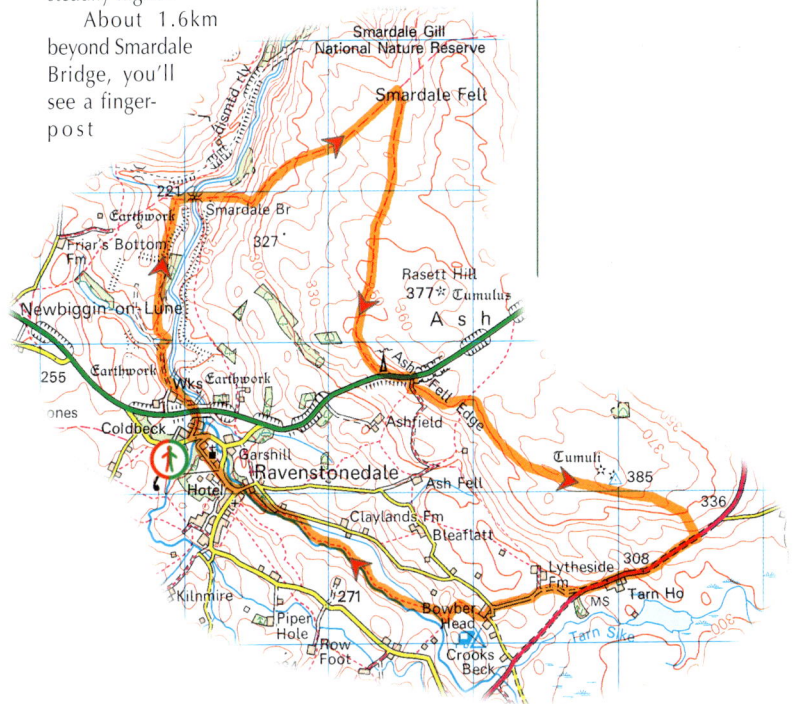

About 1.6km beyond Smardale Bridge, you'll see a fingerpost

Smardale Bridge

on the left. Turn sharp right here – signposted A685. Keep to the clearest, most obvious path as it heads generally south across **Smardale Fell**. It briefly swings slightly right of its previous line beyond a gate in a wall. Before long, the northern Howgills appear: big, rounded, grassy fells that are just crying out to be climbed.

Eventually, you walk with a wall on your right. Beyond the next gate, follow the wall down to a mast beside the **A685**. Carefully cross over and turn left. After 180m, as you draw level with the crash barrier to the left of the road, keep close to the wall on the right as it climbs away from the road. At a fingerpost in a few more metres, go through the gap in the wall – signposted Bleaflatt Lane and Lytheside.

Walking southeast, follow the wall on your left as it heads out along **Ash Fell Edge**. With close-cropped grass underfoot and the ground gently dropping away to the right, you'll feel like you're floating along. The limestone outcrops at your feet provide some foreground interest, but it is the backdrop that is truly captivating: over to the right, the Howgills still call, while to the southeast, the massive bulk of Wild Boar Fell makes its presence felt. As

WALK 4 – SMARDALE FELL AND ASH FELL EDGE

you round a slight bend, Mallerstang Edge also appears: alluring in its own wild way.

The highest point on the edge is Windy Hill, but the trig pillar is hidden from view on the other side of the wall.

Continue beside the wall until you reach the **A683**. Turn right and then, just after **Tarn House**, take the next lane on the right. You could simply follow this road back into **Ravenstonedale**, but it's more pleasant to use the meadow paths. To do this, take the next turning on the left. When the lane bends sharp left, go through the gate on the right.

Follow the track between the buildings of **Bowber Head**. As it opens out into Cumbria Classic Coaches' yard, go through the gate on the left. An enclosed path heads downhill and over a bridge. Keep straight ahead – through a metal gate on to a slightly overgrown stretch of path. Beyond the next gate, you enter a field.

Ignoring a small gate in a short while, walk with the wall on your left. Cross a footbridge and go through a gated stile. Go straight across this narrow field and then turn right to walk with the fence/wall on your left.

The route now crosses several fields. The path isn't clear on the ground; simply keep close to the field boundaries on your left and you can't go wrong. A series of small gates and stiles allows you to pass unhindered from one enclosure to the next.

Eventually, the route crosses a rough track, goes through a stile and crosses a footbridge on the right. Turn left at the road and, in another 45m, take the footpath signposted to **Ravenstonedale** on the left.

Follow **Scandal Beck** downstream and then go through a couple of wall stiles to reach a lane. Turn left here and then right at the road through the village. As this swings right near the old school, take the lane on the left – effectively straight on. The King's Head is on the right at the far end of this lane.

WALKING IN CUMBRIA'S EDEN VALLEY

WALK 5
Crosby Garrett Fell and Smardale Gill

Start/finish	Small parking area close to the entrance of Smardale Hall, about 1.8km southeast of Crosby Garrett (NY 738 082)
Distance	7 miles (11.5km)
Total ascent	342m (1122ft)
Grade	2–3
Time	3¾hr
Terrain	Quiet road; rough tracks; grassy fell; field paths; disused railway
Maps	OS Explorer OL19 or OS Landranger 91
Transport	None
Facilities	Pubs and cafés in nearby Kirkby Stephen

Rolling limestone grassland, far-reaching views, a sprawling prehistoric settlement, a National Nature Reserve and the impressive Smardale Gill Viaduct are some of the many highlights on this varied walk. Starting with a stroll along country lanes, the route gently climbs via walled tracks on to the open moorland of Crosby Garrett Fell. After briefly joining the route of Wainwright's Coast to Coast, it drops on to a disused railway through beautiful Smardale Gill, famed for its rare butterfly and wildflower species.

From the parking area, head back on to the minor road and turn left. Cross the footbridge over **Scandal Beck** and then follow the road up into **Crosby Garrett**. On reaching a road junction in the village, go straight over to cross the small bridge. Turn left and immediately right. Follow this lane round to the right, heading steadily uphill.

The public road ends at the gate to Station House. Go left here – along a rough track over the Settle–Carlisle Railway. Bear left at an early fork and then, when the track reaches a gate, bear right along a grassy path between drystone walls. Known as Ladle Lane, this gently climbing route provides great views of the North Pennines.

WALK 5 – CROSBY GARRETT FELL AND SMARDALE GILL

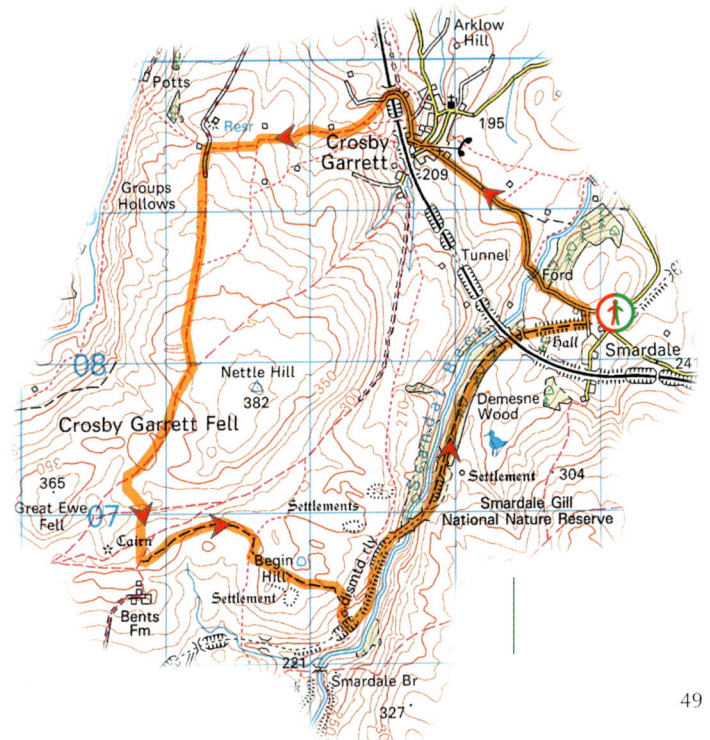

On Crosby Garrett Fell

49

Hay meadows at the foot of Crosby Garrett Fell

At a sharp left bend, go through the gate on the right and continue west, walking parallel with a wall on your left. Go through a large metal gate and turn left along a broad track.

The gate at the top of this track provides access to the open moorland of **Crosby Garrett Fell**. Once through it, keep close to the wall on the right at first – signposted Brownber. When this bends sharp right, you'll see two grassy tracks continuing straight ahead (south). Take either of these: they soon reunite close to a limestone outcrop. When they part company again in a few more metres, bear left.

On a grey, overcast day, this vast expanse of fell can seem rather dull, but with the sun shining and the larks singing, striding out easily along the close-cropped turf is pure delight. To the right, beyond the limestone pavement, the Lake District's eastern fells can be clearly seen; behind you are the North Pennines; and, after cresting a small rise, the Howgills appear ahead.

Soon after a gate in a fence, bear left at a fork. As you lose height, Wild Boar Fell and Mallerstang Edge become visible. When the ground drops away more steeply, you'll see **Bents Farm** below. ◄

Bents Farm is home to a camping barn that is popular with Coast to Coast walkers keen to break up the long day from Shap to Kirkby Stephen.

Head down the slope, still following the track at first. There's a plethora of paths in this area: use any of them to make your way to the intake wall above the farm.

On reaching the wall, turn left, now following the route of Wainwright's Coast to Coast. On reaching a kink in the wall, and just before it starts heading uphill to the left, go through a gate in it. Keep close to the new wall on your right and then cross it in 300m to continue with it on your left.

> The area to your right contains the earthwork remains of a village known as **Severals**, one of the most extensive prehistoric settlements found in Britain. The complex of huts, dykes, paths and enclosures covers about 1.2 hectares but, when combined with two other settlements just to the north, extends to about 40 hectares.

Watch your footing as you head down the next slope: there's some exposed limestone in this area and it can get slippery in wet weather. Drop to an abandoned building and follow the waymarked permissive route to the right. About 120m beyond the building, bear left to cross a bridge over a disused railway. Turn right and immediately cross the wooden stile on your right to drop on to the disused line. Turn right along the railway.

> This section of the **South Durham and Lancashire Union Railway**, also known as the Stainmore Railway, opened in 1861, and the kilns that you pass in a short while supplied lime to the steelworks in both Darlington and Barrow. The primary purpose of the railway was to take coke from County Durham to the iron and steel furnaces of Barrow and west Cumbria. The line was axed in 1962, soon after the Barrow steelworks closed.

Before long you find yourself on the massive Smardale Gill Viaduct, looking down on Scandal Beck far

Smardale Gill Viaduct

The 14-arch Smardale Gill Viaduct is 30m tall and is a listed building. For a better sense of its scale, briefly walk along the path to the right immediately after crossing it.

below. ◄ Follow the old railway line northeast as it enters woodland.

You're now in the **Smardale Gill National Nature Reserve**, which consists mostly of limestone grassland and these woods. It is home to rare plants including several types of orchid and the nationally rare bird's-foot sedge. Two important butterfly species are also found here: the northern brown argus and the Scotch argus. It is one of only two sites in England where a population of the latter may be found.

The railway path ends at the parking area near **Smardale Hall** where the walk started.

WALK 6
The Infant Eden and Pendragon Castle

Start/finish	Parish church in Kirkby Stephen (NY 775 088)
Distance	9 miles (14.5km)
Total ascent	346m (1135ft)
Grade	2
Time	4½hr
Terrain	Road through town; riverside paths; field paths; paths along base of open fell
Maps	OS Explorer OL19 or OS Landranger 91
Transport	The walk passes within 800m of Kirkby Stephen station, which is on the Settle–Carlisle Railway
Facilities	Variety of pubs and cafés in Kirkby Stephen; public toilets behind Market Square

This gentle walk starts from the attractive market town of Kirkby Stephen. It heads upstream beside the River Eden as far as the romantic ruins of Pendragon Castle, passing some fascinating rock formations along the way and then entering more rugged country as the valley narrows. The return route heads for slightly higher ground before dropping back down to the Eden.

From the church in **Kirkby Stephen**, head south along the main road. Turn left at the traffic lights, towards Nateby and Hawes. Continue for a few metres when the pavement ends, but then turn left along a path signposted to Stenkrith.

> This is Kirkby Stephen's excellent **Poetry Path**, featuring 12 short poems by local poet Meg Peacocke, all beautifully carved into a series of stones. As people walk the path they progress through the farming year, each poem depicting a different month. The first of the poems is at the end of this track.

The force of the water has carved the bed of the River Eden into unusual shapes

The bedrock here is unusual; it is made of brockram, a mixture of limestone and sandstone fragments cemented together to form a breccia.

Ignoring the bridge, turn right along the riverside path. Before long, you reach a particularly interesting section of the **River Eden**, where the water has carved the bedrock into weird and wonderful shapes. Keep to the main path as it briefly climbs away from the river and reaches a gate at the road.

It's worth taking a short detour to the Millennium Bridge by taking the path on your left before the gate. This provides a great view down into the gorge. ◀

When you're ready, return to the road and turn left. Just before the bridge, go through the gate on your right and descend the steps to the swirling river. The hard-surfaced path ends at a gate into a campsite. Just before this, bear left to continue beside the River Eden. Choose the higher of the two paths, and you'll soon be walking beside a fence. After two stiles in quick succession, turn left. When the fence kinks left, aim slightly right of your previous line to reach a stile (damaged at the time of writing) on the far side of this large field. This is quickly followed by a tiny beck and a second stile. Head straight across two small fields and through a gate.

Cross the track and go through the small gate opposite. Bear half-left, passing to the right of an old tree and through a gate in a wall above the farm buildings. With **Wharton Hall** below, continue in roughly the same direction and through another gate. Turn left along the

WALK 6 – THE INFANT EDEN AND PENDRAGON CASTLE

concrete track and right at the next junction. Keep right at a fork and then, after a cattle grid, go through the large gate over to the left. Walk south-southeast across this field and through a large gate. The next two narrower enclosures are crossed via wooden gates. After the second one, briefly swing south-southwest to pass to the right of a small mound and then aim for **Lammerside Castle** (see Walk 1 for details). After a gate, the route heads to the left of the 12th-century ruins and drops to another gate.

Once through this, turn left on an open track skirting the base of **Birkett Common** through Mallerstang. It later passes a lime kiln.

You will see a lot of **lime kilns** throughout the Eden Valley. Limestone was once burned with locally extracted coal or wood, or locally produced charcoal, to produce lime for the fields. It is used to counteract excessive acidity in the soil and enables crops to be grown on marginal land. The lime would also have been used to make mortar for building and whitewash for painting walls.

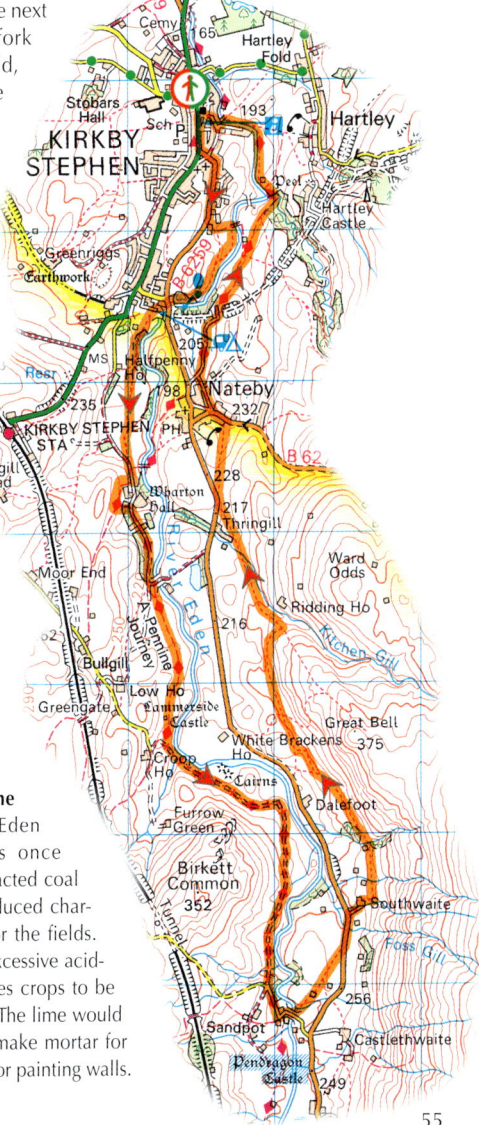

55

WALKING IN CUMBRIA'S EDEN VALLEY

Pendragon Castle is closely associated with the legend of King Arthur

At the road turn left. Just after crossing the River Eden, you will see your onward path signposted to the left, but continue along the road for now to visit **Pendragon Castle**. The castle is on private land, but it can be accessed through a gate on your right at the next road junction.

PENDRAGON CASTLE

Once three storeys high, Pendragon Castle was built in about 1160, possibly by the 12th-century knight Sir Hugh de Morville, the Lord of Westmorland, who we'll come across again in Walk 12. Local legend has it that Uther Pendragon, the father of King Arthur, originally established a castle here long before the Normans, although there is no physical evidence for this. He and dozens of his men are said to have been killed here when Saxon invaders poisoned the castle well. There is also a suggestion that he tried to divert the nearby River Eden to form a moat around the castle.

Like several other castles in Westmorland, Pendragon eventually came into the possession of the wealthy Clifford family. It was wrecked by fire and then rebuilt twice: first by Scottish raiders in the mid 14th century and then in 1541. It was left in ruins for some time after the second fire; it was only when Lady Anne Clifford came along in the middle of the 17thcentury that it was fully restored. She added stables, a brew house and a bake house. Today, the ruins include a Norman keep, a 14th-century turret and some of Lady Anne Clifford's 17th-century additions.

Walk 6 – The Infant Eden and Pendragon Castle

Walking through hay meadows near Pendragon Castle

Having explored the ruins, return to the bridge and turn right. Aim to the left of the small, ruined building ahead, crossing one stile along the way. Go through a gate in the wall to the left of the building and cross to a short section of wall in the fence ahead. Cross the stile in it and, continuing in roughly the same direction, drop to the **B6259**.

Turn left at the road, and after about 150m turn right along a farm lane. After one building, swing left and go through the right-hand of the two gates ahead. Don't be tempted by the muddy track heading through the gate straight ahead; instead, staying within the beckside enclosure for now, veer right and climb to a gate in the top wall. Immediately turn left, crossing a small gully, and head north. A fenced gill is crossed about 75m to the right of a tiny stone building. After the wall stile, keep close to the fence on the right. Just before the slope ahead steepens, dropping to Carr House, go through the small gate on the right and drop left to another gate. Keep close to the fence on the left through the trees. After fording a beck, the trail becomes slightly clearer. Nearing a large gate, bear right to cross a gated stile. The path keeps close to the wall on the left. After the next gate, stay with the wall until it drops more steeply to the left. Keep right here and then right again on joining a path from the left. Bear left at a fork.

Close to the ruined buildings at **Ridding House**, cross a stile next to a gate on your left and then follow Thringill Beck downstream to a railed footbridge. Cross this and go through the small gate. Turn left to walk beside the wall/fence at first and then aim for the metal gate on the other side of the field. Once through this, walk with the wall on your left, through another gate in the far corner and then beside the wall on the right. Reaching a gate in this wall, swing left across the field to another gate.

Turn right along the **B6259** and, almost immediately, enter the layby on the right. Go through the easy-to-miss gated stile in the wall (next to a wooden gate). Walk with the fence/wall on your left. Having gone through a small gate, head left to go through a second one. Now walk between two rows of trees to access a walled path.

Turn left at the road, into **Nateby**, and then right down a surfaced lane. Cross any one of the small bridges on your right to continue with the stream on your left. Follow a walled track – signposted Hartley Lane – to a T-junction and turn right. Having followed this track for 1km, ignore a path to Kirkby Stephen on the left.

After the next bridge, keep left to walk along the banks of the **River Eden**. Cross Frank's Bridge on the edge of **Kirkby Stephen** and quickly bear right to climb the steps between the buildings. Turn right at the top and follow the lane back up to the church.

> The attractive red sandstone parish church, known locally as the **Cathedral of the Dales**, is well worth a visit. The earliest stone church on the site, part of which can still be seen, dates from the late 12th century. Among the interesting relics inside is the eighth-century Loki Stone, one of only two such stones in Europe representing the Norse god.

WALK 7
Kirkby Stephen to Appleby

Start	Kirkby Stephen railway station (NY 761 067)
Finish	Appleby-in-Westmorland railway station (NY 686 206)
Distance	15 miles (24km)
Total ascent	509m (1670ft)
Grade	3
Time	6½hr
Terrain	Limestone grassland; riverside meadows; field paths; woodland
Maps	OS Explorer OL19 or OS Landranger 91
Transport	The start and finish are both on the Settle–Carlisle railway
Facilities	Variety of pubs and cafés in Appleby

This may be a long walk, but it is by no means hard. Another linear route linking stations on the Settle–Carlisle railway, it meanders through pretty countryside in the Upper Eden Valley, perfect for a long, hot summer's day. Crossing limestone uplands to the east of Kirkby Stephen, it then descends to beckside meadows as it follows Scandal Beck downstream to Soulby. Farm paths and tracks then lead to Warcop where you pick up the River Eden, the route of which is followed all the way to Appleby.

Leave **Kirkby Stephen station** and head to the main road, along which you turn right. After about 800m, as you reach the Kirkby Stephen town sign, turn left up a track – signposted Ashfell. Beyond the gate at the top, enter a narrow belt of woodland via a ladder stile in the left-hand corner. Walk with a fence on your left. After leaving the trees, continue beside the fence and cross a stile in a wall. Heading slightly left of your previous line, walk under the railway, passing the earthwork remains of a long-abandoned settlement along the way.

Continue southwest, soon picking up the line of a wall on your right for a short while, but then

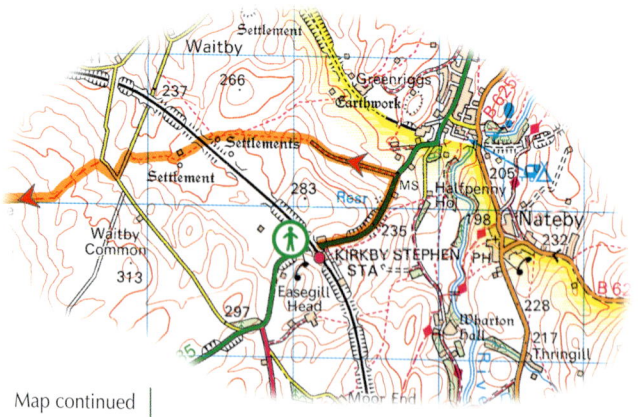

Map continued on page 61

The fortified manor house of Smardale Hall was built in the 15th and 16th centuries on the site of an older building.

swinging left to cross a stile at the other end of the field. Turn left along the road and then right at the T-junction. When this road bends right, go through the gate on the left – signposted Brownber.

For the next 1.1km, keep close to the wall on the right, ignoring any paths tempting you away from it. Having dropped to a wall corner, go through the gate on the right. Head downhill with a wall on your left at first.

Beyond the next gate, aim for the turrets of **Smardale Hall** directly below. ◄

Crossing open fell at the start of the walk

WALK 7 – KIRKBY STEPHEN TO APPLEBY

Pick up a rough track beside a wall which drops to a gate beside a cottage at **Smardale**. Go through to join a lane. Turn left at the T-junction and follow the road round to the left, towards Crosby Garrett. Immediately after the **Scandal Beck** ford and bridge, take the path on the right – signposted Smardale Mill. It crosses a stile and continues through beckside meadows beside the fence on your right. Having crossed a stile next to a bridge over Scandal Beck, go straight over the sunken track and cross the stile opposite. Go through the gate on the right and turn left. The fence on your left is your guide until you reach the next set of buildings. After a stile to the right of the buildings, cross the lane diagonally left to find a camouflaged stile in a wall. Cross this to continue beckside.

Map continued on page 63

Nearing some more buildings, cross a stile on the right and keep close to the beck. Reaching a surfaced lane, turn right. Turn right at the road and then left at the crossroads in **Soulby**, towards Appleby. When the road bends left a few hundred metres beyond the last buildings, turn right along a gravel track.

Beyond the buildings at **Sykeside**, the track ends close to a small farm shed. The right-of-way continues through a metal gate beside a tiny beck to the left of this building. Now walk with the fence and beck on your left and go through a gate.

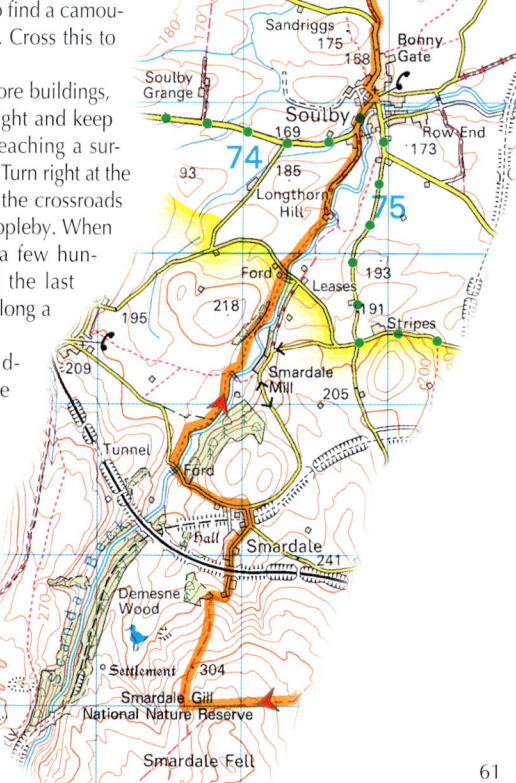

WALKING IN CUMBRIA'S EDEN VALLEY

Walk between two fences. Entering an area of damp pasture, keep straight ahead to cross a stile. Continue in the same direction (north-northeast) across another stile. Pass between the field boundary on your left and the building up to your right to reach a track. Bear left along this to drop to a gate beside the road.

Turn right and then immediately left, over a small bridge and stile. Keep close to the fence on your right until you reach a gate. Beyond this, continue in the same direction with a tiny beck on your left. Having crossed a stile and bridge, turn right to walk beside the beck, which soon swings left.

Keep to the left of the fenced pond. Follow this fence round to a gate. Go through this and, joining the Pennine Journey long-distance path, turn left along a concrete track for about 100m. Cross a stile and bridge on the left, and follow the tiny beck upstream for a few metres. After one small gate, go through the next one on the right. Now head uphill beside the hedgerow.

After the stile at the top of the rise, follow the rough track through the gate straight ahead, enjoying good views towards the North Pennines above Warcop. ◄

After a gate just above the river, keep close to the fence on the right. Having dropped to the water's edge, follow the river to the road on the edge of **Warcop**.

> Don't be too alarmed if you hear automatic gunfire or explosions in this area; the Army's Warcop firing ranges are just to the north.

Warcop is one of the few villages in Cumbria that still holds an annual rush-bearing festival. The custom dates from the time when church floors were compacted mud and had to be strewn with rushes. (This also helped to mask the smell of any shallow burials beneath the church.) Every year, the old rushes were removed and replaced with fresh ones.

The earthen floor disappeared many decades ago, but the tradition lives on in Warcop as well as in four other Cumbrian villages: Ambleside, Grasmere, Urswick and Great Musgrave. Warcop's ceremony usually takes place on St Peter's Day, 29 June.

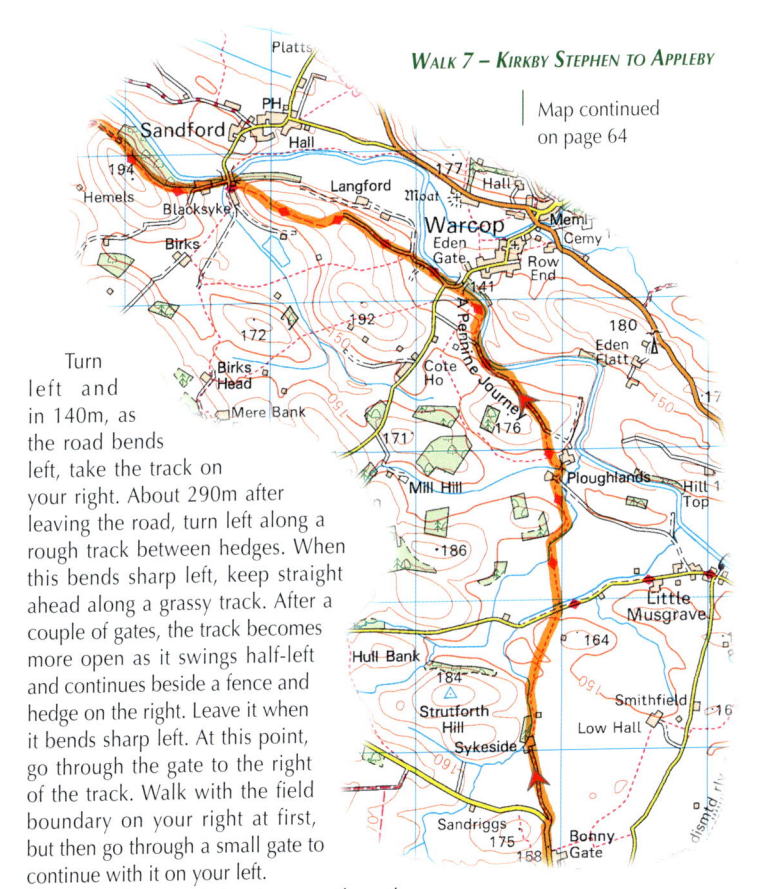

WALK 7 – KIRKBY STEPHEN TO APPLEBY

Map continued on page 64

Turn left and in 140m, as the road bends left, take the track on your right. About 290m after leaving the road, turn left along a rough track between hedges. When this bends sharp left, keep straight ahead along a grassy track. After a couple of gates, the track becomes more open as it swings half-left and continues beside a fence and hedge on the right. Leave it when it bends sharp left. At this point, go through the gate to the right of the track. Walk with the field boundary on your right at first, but then go through a small gate to continue with it on your left.

At the bottom of the slope, go through the small gate to the left of the bungalow. Turn right and quickly left along a track towards the farm at **Blacksyke**. As the line of buildings on the right ends, bear half-right through a wooden gate to the right of a metal silo – signposted Little Ormside. Walk gently uphill between a hedge and some woodland. After a small gate, descend with a fence on your right, soon picking up a track that takes you to **Little Ormside**.

Follow the road past all the buildings and continue to **Great Ormside**. At the junction on the edge of the

63

WALKING IN CUMBRIA'S EDEN VALLEY

Cross Tree, Great Ormside

Map continued on page 65

village, go straight over to pick up a rough track. Bear left when this forks. After passing under the railway, cross a ladder stile. Walk with the fence on your left and then swing left along a narrow strip of land. At the bottom of the slope, bear right and head downhill. After the next stile, a muddy trail drops into **Jeremy Gill**. Cross the footbridge. After climbing the slope on the other side, cross a stile on the right. The clear path through the woods later swings right, down some steps to the riverbank.

You now follow this riverside route practically all the way to Appleby. Sometimes you are in woodland, sometimes in fields, but always following the **River Eden** downstream. After 1.9km on the riverside path, nearing Appleby, you pass through a large field. As it narrows, cross the stile in the left-hand corner. A path beside a fence now leads to a lane behind **Appleby Castle**. Turn left here and then right at the T-junction.

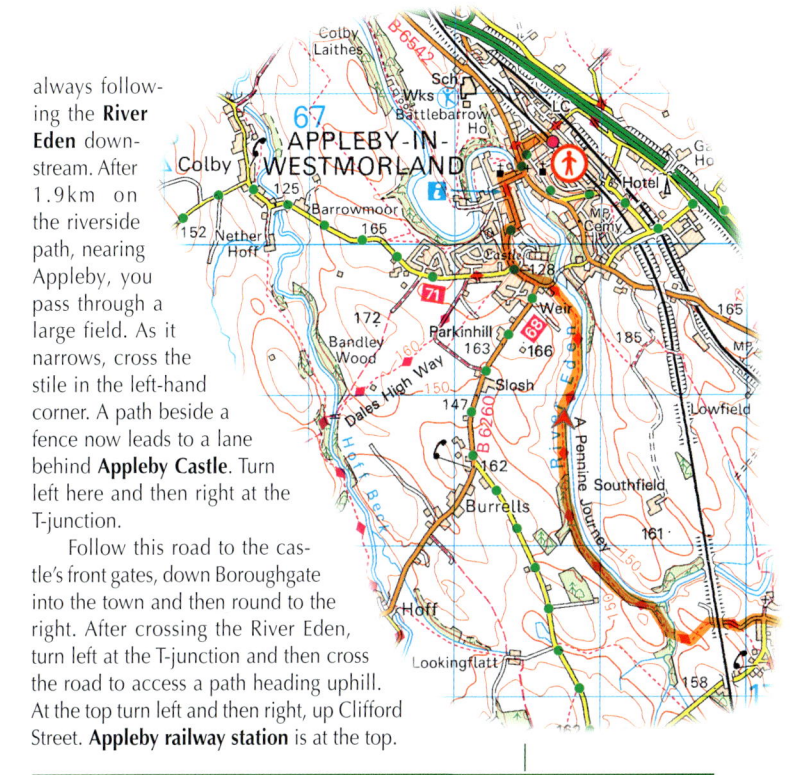

Follow this road to the castle's front gates, down Boroughgate into the town and then round to the right. After crossing the River Eden, turn left at the T-junction and then cross the road to access a path heading uphill. At the top turn left and then right, up Clifford Street. **Appleby railway station** is at the top.

APPLEBY-IN-WESTMORLAND

Appleby is definitely worth exploring if you have time before your train. It developed as a market town soon after the Norman Conquest, its charter dating back to 1174. The castle also dates from Norman times, and although much of it was rebuilt in the 17th century, the splendid keep, known as Caesar's Tower, is 12th century.

Like many castles in the area, and other buildings in Appleby, it owes its continuing existence to the efforts of Lady Anne Clifford, a strong-willed and passionate member of the local aristocracy during the 17th century. She was born in Skipton Castle in 1590, the sole heir of the third earl of Cumberland. She failed to inherit her father's Westmorland estates on his death; they eventually passed to her uncle and then her cousin. She fought hard to regain

WALKING IN CUMBRIA'S EDEN VALLEY

what was rightfully hers and even made a direct, although unsuccessful, appeal to the king. Eventually, her cousin died without a male heir and Lady Anne won back her estates.

On the death of her second husband she moved into Appleby Castle and began a massive project, restoring her castles at Brough, Brougham and Pendragon.

Every June the tranquillity of this peaceful town is shattered as thousands of Romany families, some in colourful, horse-drawn caravans, arrive for the centuries-old horse fair, the largest of its kind in the world.

St Anne's Hospital in Appleby is a group of almshouses founded by Lady Anne Clifford for poor widows in the mid-17th century

WALK 8
Great Asby Scar

Start/finish	Market Hall in Orton village (NY 622 082)
Distance	8¾ miles (14km)
Total ascent	324m (1063ft)
Grade	2–3
Time	4½hr
Terrain	Field paths, muddy in places; quiet lanes; tracks; grassy paths across limestone pavement
Maps	OS Explorer OL19 or OS Landranger 91
Transport	Bus 106
Facilities	George Hotel, Kennedy's Chocolate Factory and Orton Scar Café, all in Orton

Great Asby Scar contains one of the most extensive and pristine areas of limestone pavement in Britain. Its clints and grikes (see Geology in the Introduction), as well as the surrounding grasslands, are home to a diverse range of birds and often rare plants. Walkers setting out on this route from the lovely village of Orton will also be treated to superb, ever-changing views – one minute the Howgills, the next the North Pennines and, finally, the eastern Lake District fells.

Opposite Orton's Market Hall is the Coronation Shelter. Head left of this to join a surfaced path past a play area. Cross the road to gain the walled trail opposite. After a tiny stile – and with the Howgills to the right – walk beside the wall on the left across several fields.

On reaching a road – Street Lane – turn left. After 180m, cross the stile on the right. Walk with the wall on your right. After a dip, the path passes through a wall gap to continue in the same direction – sometimes with a wall on your left, sometimes on the right. Drop to another gap, cross a bridge and then swing right to walk beside an old hedgerow. When this ends, keep straight on, aiming for the farm at **Scarside**.

Turn right along the lane in front of the farmhouse. After the last building, cross the stile on the left. Walk roughly parallel with the fence on the left and then leave the field via a stile beside a metal gate. Cross the track and tackle the stile opposite.

Now following Wainwright's Coast to Coast route and heading east in an almost straight line for 1.3km, walk across several fields with a series of gates/stiles and occasional waymarkers guiding you. You have the wall on your right at first but then pass through a gate/stile to continue with it on your left. Then, soon after an old barn, you lose the line of the wall, but the route remains obvious as it crosses stiles and passes through gates. The route ahead is less clear as you enter the penultimate meadow – now aim for the small clump of sycamores immediately ahead. After passing through a gate next to the trees, make for the building at **Acres** straight ahead.

Turn left along the lane in front of the house. As the road bends right near the next set of dwellings at **Sunbiggin**, take the track on the left – signposted Great Asby. This soon passes to the left of some farm buildings.

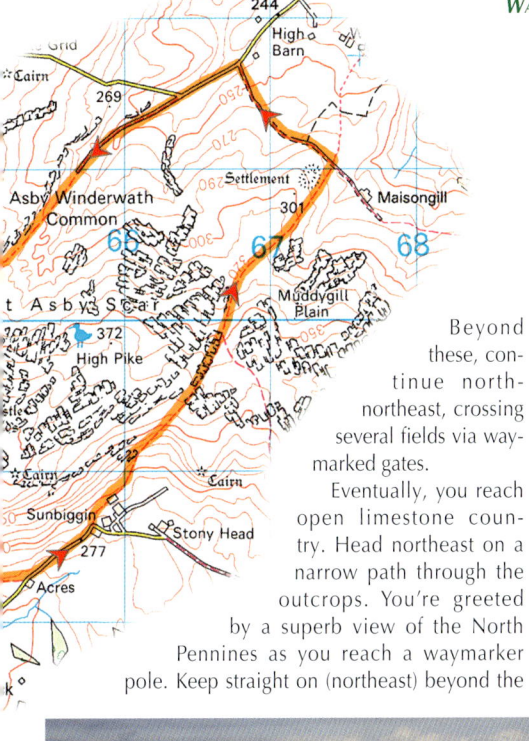

WALK 8 – GREAT ASBY SCAR

Beyond these, continue north-northeast, crossing several fields via waymarked gates.

Eventually, you reach open limestone country. Head northeast on a narrow path through the outcrops. You're greeted by a superb view of the North Pennines as you reach a waymarker pole. Keep straight on (northeast) beyond the

The long line of the North Pennines stretches into the distance as you reach the highest point on the walk

69

Looking back down Copper Mine Lane

pole – towards a small gate in a wall. Go through to walk beside the fence on your right. Go through the next gate and then, a few metres later, go through a gate on the right. Turn left beside the fence. Go through the gate in the next wall and follow the indistinct path, keeping close to the wall on the right. Eventually, having passed through several gates, you reach a vehicle track, where you turn left. (The last field contains earthwork traces of a Romano-British settlement.)

Turn left at the road. Then, at a right-hand bend, turn left up a track known as Copper Mine Lane. When this ends, go through the gate and walk with the wall on your left. A few metres beyond the next gate, bear right – uphill to go through a small gate.

Follow the narrow, but clear path southwest through **Great Asby Scar National Nature Reserve**, skirting the edge of the limestone pavement at first but then climbing straight through the middle of this fascinating scenery.

> Grazing has been stopped on **Great Asby Scar NNR** to allow dwarf trees and deep heather to grow. The area is home to a number of rare plants, including Solomon's seal, rigid buckler fern and both black

WALK 8 – GREAT ASBY SCAR

Crossing Great Asby Scar

and green spleenwort ferns, although you may have to peer deep into the grikes to see them.

Turn left at a T-junction, and climb to a gate. Once through this, a clear path on close-cropped grass leads to a crossing of routes at a fingerpost. ▶

Continue straight on, ignoring the gate near the fingerpost, but then go through the gate in the fence just below. Cross the field diagonally right, through a small gate in a wall. Following roughly the same bearing, you'll pass a fingerpost on the hillside and go through another small gate with a yellow-topped post beside it. Walk parallel with the wall for about 180m and then drop left to go through a gate.

Cut diagonally across the next field and through a large gate. Walking in the same direction, you'll reach a small gate in the wall opposite. Follow the enclosed path to its end and then bear left to reach a surfaced lane – Street Lane again.

Turn right and walk along the asphalt for about 1km. Cross the awkward gated stile in the wall on your right to retrace your steps into **Orton**, walking beside the field boundary on your right and then crossing a quiet lane to pick up the surfaced path back into the village.

> The distant views have changed yet again, now encompassing the eastern Lake District.

WALKING IN CUMBRIA'S EDEN VALLEY

WALK 9
Potts Valley and the Orton Fells

Start/finish	Informal roadside parking on fell road linking Raisbeck with Little Asby and Whygill Head. Park near cattle grid above Sunbiggin Tarn (NY 675 077)
Distance	11 miles (18km)
Total ascent	399m (1309ft)
Grade	2–3
Time	5hr
Terrain	Paths and tracks across low moorland; field paths; quiet roads; grassy valley path, wet in places
Maps	OS Explorer OL19 or OS Landranger 91
Transport	None
Facilities	George Hotel, Kennedy's Chocolate Factory and Orton Scar Café, all in Orton, 6.1km west of the starting point

The highlight of this walk is Potts Valley – undoubtedly one of Cumbria's best-kept secrets. This divine dale is hidden away between the limestone pavement of Little Asby Scar and the open grassland of Crosby Garrett Fell. The crystal clear waters of Potts Beck flow through verdant pastures, towered over by impressive limestone outcrops. But this walk is about much more than just this gorgeous valley. It crosses a corner of Great Asby Scar's extensive and fascinating limestone pavement; it saunters over the wildflower-rich grassland of Ravenstonedale Moor; and, throughout, it enjoys ever-changing views... One minute you're looking into the steep-sided valleys cutting through the Howgills; next, you're feeling the might of the North Pennines bearing down on the scene; and then, having turned another corner, you're gazing across to the Lake District.

From the cattle grid above **Sunbiggin Tarn**, walk south-west along the road for about 200m and you'll see an 'access land' information panel on the right. Turn right here – signposted Coast to Coast. As you cross Tarn Moor, about 150m from the road, a damp area is reached. Don't

WALK 9 – POTTS VALLEY AND THE ORTON FELLS

be tempted by the path heading uphill here; instead, swing left and keep to the base of the slope. The route becomes more obvious as it climbs slightly and swings right. At a faint crossing of tracks, keep straight ahead. (The Coast to Coast goes left here, while our route continues on the less-walked Dales High Way.)

Maintain a straight line to reach a gate in a wall. Go through this and head steadily uphill beside a wall. There's no path at first, but as you reach the first significant limestone outcrops, you'll join a broad, grassy track heading in your direction. When this forks, keep left, staying with the wall.

After a gate, the track disappears, but you should continue following the wall. You finally part company with it when it bends left; continue north-northwest. The path becomes more obvious as it drops. ▶

Nearing the point at which a fence and wall meet, descend the pathless ground to reach a small gate at the wall corner. Go through this and then walk with the wall on your right. Passing through several gates along the way, you'll reach a farm track. Turn right here – signposted Whygill Head.

Ponies grazing on Tarn Moor

Looking across the vast silvery expanse of limestone pavement to the left, you can see the Lake District fells. Straight ahead is Cross Fell.

The track passes to the right of the farm buildings at **Maisongill**. When it bends left after the last shed, keep straight on – through a gate. Follow the fence on the right and then go through another gate. Veer left towards a wall and walk beside this. As it heads downhill and kinks left, go through the large gate straight ahead. Walk straight across the next meadow (east) to the next gate. (This is not the gate in the field corner.) Once through this, walk beside the wall on the left. Once in the next

WALK 9 – POTTS VALLEY AND THE ORTON FELLS

enclosure, veer right along a farm track that ends at a large gate. Don't go through this; instead, go through the slightly smaller gate to the left of it. Continue east beside a wall and through a small gate. After dropping into a dip, veer left to a gate in a fence. Go through this and turn right along the **Asby Grange** lane – signposted Whygill.

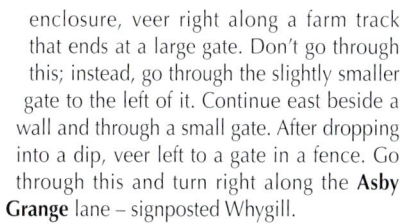

Ignore a footpath signed to the right in a few metres but then, just before the lane starts climbing, turn right along a rough track. Go through the gate and, crossing two fields connected via a wall gap, walk parallel with the wall on the left.

In the next, larger field, continue east-northeast, never veering too far from the wall on the left. You'll eventually find a gate in the northeast corner. Go through and turn left to cross some very muddy ground to reach the next gate. Once through this, turn right. Keep close to the wall and you'll eventually be channelled between that wall and a fence to another gate. Once in the next field, keep close to the fence on the left and it'll eventually lead to a gate beside the road.

Looking down Potts Valley towards the Pennine escarpment

WALKING IN CUMBRIA'S EDEN VALLEY

Potts Beck

Turn right along the asphalt. This later crosses **Potts Beck** close to **Water Houses** and then climbs the other side of the valley. About 480m after Water Houses, take the walled track rising to the right. Having followed this for about 500m, go through the large metal gate on the right – signposted Water Houses, Potts. With occasional views of the North Pennines, a field track heads downhill – beside the wall on the right at first.

The track drops into **Potts Valley** and heads upstream. Beyond the abandoned farm buildings at **Potts**, drop to the footbridge over the bubbling beck, but don't cross it. Instead, walk with the water on your right. The path makes for easy going, although it has been undercut by the beck in a couple of places.

More and more **limestone** encroaches on the scene, adding rocky drama to this otherwise placid location. The grey scars of Little Asby and Hazzler Brow can seem rather austere on a dull day, but they spring to glinting, gleaming life in the sun.

Drawing level with some ruins on the other side of the valley, the path swings away from the beck slightly. It crosses damp ground to reach a large, wooden gate. Go through this. A faint, wet path leads away from the gate and quickly joins up with a clearer path from the right. Bear left at a fork in a short while. Climbing, this broad, grassy path passes above some enclosed ground. As you reach the southwest corner of these enclosures, the right-of-way drops to the right, but our route keeps straight ahead on the broad path. It's not always obvious, but as long as you keep heading southwest across this moorland, you'll eventually reach an unfenced road. Turn left here.

After cresting a rise, the Howgills fill the vista ahead. About 500m beyond a cattle grid, you'll see a rough track to the left, leading up to a reservoir mound. Turn right here – along a broad path (west). Joining another path from the left, swing down to a gate into a walled enclosure. Don't go through this; instead, bear left to walk with the enclosure on your right. At the wall corner, keep straight on – along a path climbing the slope ahead – and then turn right along a clear path.

This forms part of Wainwright's Coast to Coast as well as the Dales High Way. It winds its way over **Ravenstonedale Moor**. A few hundred metres after crossing a bridge and going through a gate, you'll see the meandering channel of **Tarn Sike** on the right and Sunbiggin Tarn beyond that. Soon after this, bear right at a fork. Turn right at the road. The cattle grid where the walk started is less than 800m ahead.

WALK 10
Crosby Ravensworth Fell

Start/finish	Crosby Ravensworth village hall (NY 620 147)
Distance	6½ miles (10.5km)
Total ascent	253m (830ft)
Grade	2–3
Time	3½hr
Terrain	Farm paths; grassy tracks on open heather moorland
Maps	OS Explorer OL19 or OS Landranger 91
Transport	None
Facilities	Butchers' Arms in Crosby Ravensworth

This beautiful expanse of low limestone moorland is steeped in history: from ancient pre-Roman settlements to Charles I's journey south to his final, unsuccessful battle of the Civil War. The best time to visit is the late summer when the sweet smell of flowering heather fills the air and the ground is a carpet of purple.

With your back to **Crosby Ravensworth** village hall, turn right along the road and, after about 100m, go through the metal gate on the right – signposted Holme Bridge.

Winter on the limestone pavement of Crosby Ravensworth Fell

WALK 10 – CROSBY RAVENSWORTH FELL

Once through the next gate, directly ahead, walk beside the fence on the right. After the gate at the end of this track, climb the ladder stile on your right. Turn left to follow the pretty **Lyvennet Beck** upstream.

> The name '**Lyvennet**' is closely associated with the post-Roman Celtic kingdom of Rheged, which covered much of modern-day Cumbria. It is thought that Urien, who had a number of victories over Anglian chieftains in the second half of the sixth century, ruled from 'Llwyfenydd'. Urien was a descendant of Coel Han, or 'Old King Cole'. His son was Uwain, one of the kingdom's greatest heroes who inspired his men to fight rather than give tribute to the English.
>
> The stories of Rheged are steeped in myth and legend, so it is hard to talk with any certainty about 'historical facts'. Some, for instance, claim that Llwyfenydd was in Wales and the Lyvennet was merely named after it; others will tell you that Llwyfenydd and Lyvennet are, in fact, the same place.

You soon cross a wooden step stile, beyond which keep close to the fence on the left. Having crossed a stile in this fence, bear right to head towards a small gate in a wall. Once through this, turn left at the road. Immediately after the bridge, cross the two stiles on the right – signposted Crosby Lodge and Orton.

Keeping close to the field boundary on

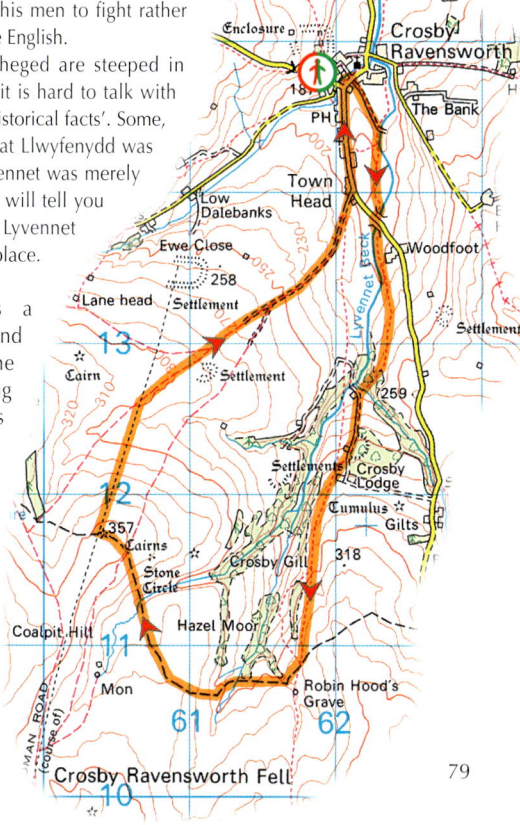

your right, cross the next wall via a stile to the right of a metal gate. Once over yet another stile you lose the guiding fence/wall on your right; head straight over to the next wall and cross the well-camouflaged stone stile to the left of the gate.

Continuing southwards, head gently uphill to the immediate left of some trees, later picking up the line of a fence. Go through the next metal gate on the right to head downhill on a track. Just beyond the gate in the bottom of the valley, turn left at a T-junction to head gently uphill. ◄

> The lines of stones and remains of hut circles to the left belong to Burwens, a settlement thought to have been inhabited by ancient Britons long before the Romans arrived.

About 100m after passing a solitary barn beside the track, cross the stile on the right. Bear left, heading for a gap in a wall to the right of the buildings at **Crosby Lodge**. Go through the gate on the right and then, in just a few strides, bear left.

After a gate next to a solitary tree, keep close to the wall on the left, later joining a rough farm track. Follow this through a gate and up to a fork, where you bear left. Once through the next gate, the vehicle track disappears; head south, straight across the field. As you approach a wall on the other side, drop to a gate where the wall meets a fence. Go through and immediately cross the gated stile on the left. ◄

> The open fell here is dotted with burial cairns, stone circles and the remains of ancient settlements.

Turn right to walk beside the wall on **Crosby Ravensworth Fell**. The path soon drops steeply into a dry valley, typical of limestone country. Once you've climbed out the other side, keep close to the fence/wall on your right. The path dips again to cross a tiny beck and then continues beside the wall. Having followed the wall for about 1km, it performs a sharp bend to the right. Leave it here by heading north-northwest along a grassy path and then ford the shallow infant **Lyvennet**.

> Just up the valley from here is the **Black Dub Monument**. Erected in 1843 close to the source of the Lyvennet, it marks the spot where, in August 1651, Charles II and his men stopped for water on their way south from Scotland. Having done a deal with the Scottish Covenanters and been crowned

WALK 10 – CROSBY RAVENSWORTH FELL

king at Scone, he had been hoping to reassert the rule of the Crown in England. His forces, however, were defeated by Cromwell's more powerful New Model Army at the Battle of Worcester on 3 September.

As the path heads uphill, keep left at any forks, following a line of wooden posts for now and passing two round boulders – probably erratics deposited by a glacier. Forking left again on the high ground, the path swings west as it skirts the southern edge of the limestone pavement – with views ahead of the eastern Lake District fells. It then gradually swings back round to the right, always keeping to the left of the outcrops. As a broad path joins from the left, you'll reach a faint junction of routes. Head north-northeast, soon passing to the left of a solitary hawthorn growing out of the limestone. As you draw level with a second, larger tree, keep left at a fork to maintain the same direction. This track follows almost the same line as Wicker Street, the Roman road linking the fort at Low Borrow Bridge on the Lune with either Brougham or Kirkby Thore. After fording a small beck, head straight up the slope on the other side.

Erratic left by a glacier

Summer on Crosby Ravensworth Fell

Nearing the top of the small rise, bear right along another wide, grassy track, heading northeast. As you stride out across the open moorland with the North Pennines directly ahead, you gradually find yourself being funnelled into an ever-narrowing strip of access land between two walls. Eventually, the grassy path becomes more solid underfoot and then joins a track from the right. On reaching the road, turn left and walk the 730m back to the village hall in **Crosby Ravensworth**.

WALK 11
*Knipescar Common and
River Lowther*

Start/finish	Bampton Memorial Hall private car park with honesty box (NY 516 181)
Distance	5¼ miles (8.5km)
Total ascent	190m (623ft)
Grade	2
Time	2½hr
Terrain	Quiet lanes; track; limestone fell; riverside path
Maps	OS Explorer OL5 or OS Landranger 90
Transport	None
Facilities	Bampton Shop and Tea Room, Mardale Inn, both in Bampton; Crown and Mitre Inn, Bampton Grange

This is the only walk in this book that strays into the Lake District National Park. It takes in Knipescar Common, a little-visited area of limestone separated from the main body of the fells by the River Lowther. It's easily climbed from the road and, once you're on the top of the limestone plateau, you'll inevitably be consumed by a desire to walk for miles on these peaceful grasslands. Sadly, they don't go on for miles, so you'll have to content yourself with a slow stroll along the edge of the escarpment, enjoying the lovely views of the Lake District and the North Pennines, before dropping to the River Lowther and a gentle amble back to Bampton. Walk the river route at dawn or dusk and there's a chance of seeing deer, badgers or even otters.

From the car park, turn left along the road. (There is an off-road path to the left of the asphalt.) Follow the road over **Haweswater Beck** and then over the **River Lowther** to enter **Bampton Grange**. Ignoring a turning to Whale and Knipe on the left, keep to the road as it climbs out of the village.

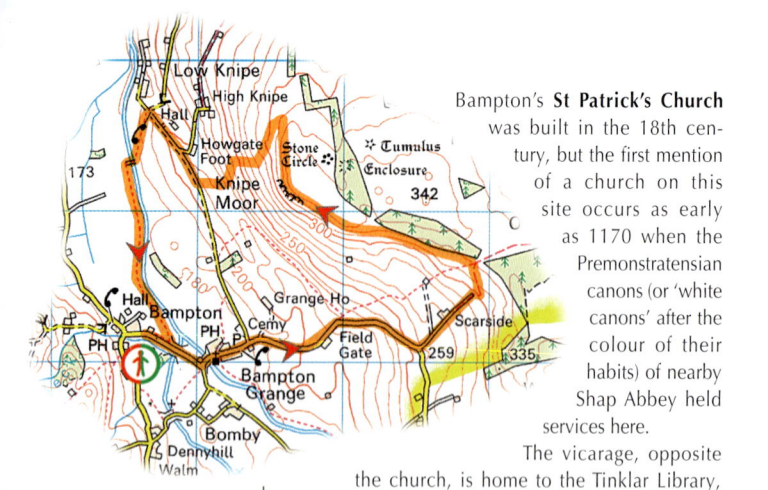

Bampton's **St Patrick's Church** was built in the 18th century, but the first mention of a church on this site occurs as early as 1170 when the Premonstratensian canons (or 'white canons' after the colour of their habits) of nearby Shap Abbey held services here.

The vicarage, opposite the church, is home to the Tinklar Library, which contains an important collection of Latin books.

About 1.5km beyond **Bampton Grange**, take the surfaced lane to **Scarside** on the left. (A fingerpost to the right of the road indicates this is a bridleway.) Beyond the buildings, keep straight on – along a rough track rising between drystone walls.

Beyond the gate at the top of the lane, as you step out on to access land, take the track climbing left. The grassy bridleway climbs to a wall. Don't go through the gate here; instead, bear left to walk with the wall on your right. This broad, grassy track later comes away from the wall as it continues along the top of Knipescar Common's limestone plateau. ◄

To the left are the Lake District's far eastern fells, including High Street. The northeastern end of Haweswater Reservoir and its dam are also briefly visible. Far to the northwest, you can see the distinctive outline of Blencathra.

There is plenty of evidence of early man on **Knipescar Common**, including a stone circle, an ancient enclosure and tumuli, although you'll need to wander from the path to find any signs of them. The lower, southwestern slopes are also home to disused quarry workings and old lime kilns.

WALK 11 – KNIPESCAR COMMON AND RIVER LOWTHER

About 500m after first encountering the wall on Knipescar Common, bear left along a faint trail, staying close to the escarpment edge. Before long, the North Pennines put in an appearance to the northeast.

On reaching a broad, grassy path, turn left. (This is about 150m short of a wall running across the ridge to the north.) Almost immediately, as a narrower path branches right, keep to the clearer path heading roughly southwest. The track briefly swings right and then, on nearing a wall, bends left again. At the bottom of this gorse- and bracken-covered slope, the way ahead is less obvious. The path swings slightly right (west) – but don't be tempted by the trail heading sharp right.

On reaching the minor road, turn right. In about 800m, as you draw level with an old red phone box (now an information kiosk), take the narrow trail on the left – signposted Bampton. Crossing some damp ground along the way, this gradually drops southwest towards the **River Lowther**.

On Knipescar Common

WALKING IN CUMBRIA'S EDEN VALLEY

Footbridge over a frozen River Lowther

A wobbly bridge is crossed. (A slightly disconcerting sign asks people not to 'gather' on the bridge and suggests it should be used by no more than two people at a time.)

Turn left through the kissing-gate to follow a lovely riverside path upstream. Most of the time, you'll have the **River Lowther** on your left, but, for the last hundred metres or so, you'll be following **Haweswater Beck**. Reaching the road, turn right to retrace your steps to the car park.

Walk 11 – Knipescar Common and River Lowther

OTTERS IN THE EDEN VALLEY

There are otters throughout the Eden catchment, and several have been seen along the River Lowther. Having been driven to the brink of extinction during the second half of the 20th century, these elusive creatures are making a dramatic comeback on Cumbria's rivers.

Otter numbers began to decline seriously in the 1950s. Although factors such as habitat loss, changes to land management, hunting and road deaths were partly to blame, the main cause seems to have been the growing use of pesticides such as dieldrin. This poison, used as a seed dressing and in sheep-dip, found its way into watercourses and fish stock. The reproductive ability of otters, feeding on the contaminated fish, was severely impaired. Only as dieldrin was slowly withdrawn from use, and then banned entirely in 1989, did otter numbers begin to recover.

You need to be both quiet and patient if you want to see an otter; they are notoriously difficult to spot. Keep your eyes peeled for their prints in the soft mud on the riverbank. Otters have five webbed toes, although it is common for only four to show up in prints; the rear paw print tends to be longer. Also watch for holes in the bank, especially near trees with large root systems, or for piles of sticks and brambles at the edge of the water; these could indicate an entrance to a holt. Otters tend not to dig their own homes, they will use natural holes or even old rabbit burrows.

Solitary male otters and family groups have their own territories, which they mark by leaving smelly droppings, or spraints, in prominent locations such as on large boulders or at the base of tree trunks. Spraints tend to be black and tarry, containing a lot of fish bones, but the only sure-fire way of recognising an otter spraint is to sniff it; its smell has been variously described as fishy or like freshly mown hay, jasmine tea or lavender.

WALKING IN CUMBRIA'S EDEN VALLEY

WALK 12
River Lyvennet at King's Meaburn

Start/finish	White Horse Inn, King's Meaburn (NY 620 212)
Distance	6¼ miles (10km)
Total ascent	204m (670ft)
Grade	2
Time	3hr
Terrain	Field and riverside paths, including badly eroded section; quiet lanes and tracks
Maps	OS Explorer OL19 or OS Landranger 91
Transport	None
Facilities	White Horse Inn, King's Meaburn

This gentle stroll follows the River Lyvennet as it meanders its way through woods and meadows close to King's Meaburn. The route then heads away from the water, ambling along quiet country lanes, tracks and bridleways through pleasant, gently rolling countryside with good views of both the Pennines and the Lake District fells.

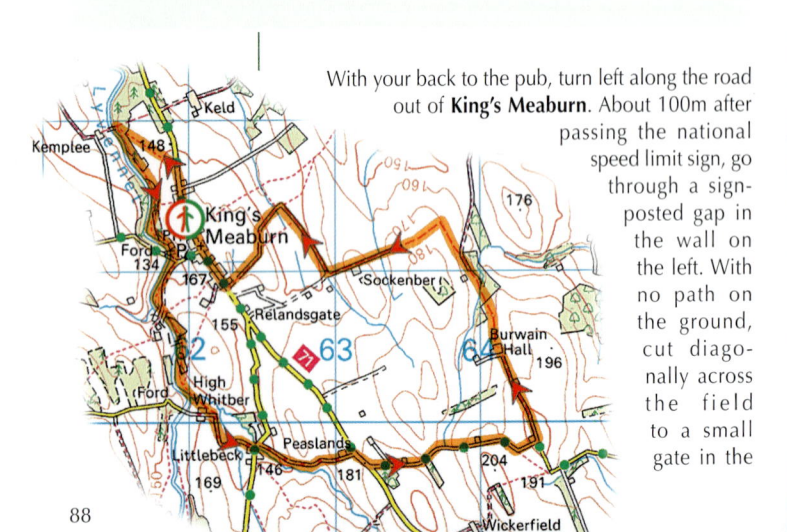

With your back to the pub, turn left along the road out of **King's Meaburn**. About 100m after passing the national speed limit sign, go through a sign-posted gap in the wall on the left. With no path on the ground, cut diagonally across the field to a small gate in the hedges. Continue in the same direction through the next two fields.

Enter the woods via a stile close to the field corner and follow the trail down through the trees to a track and a bridge over the **River Lyvennet**. Don't cross; instead, turn left along a path beside the river. Passing through gates and climbing stiles along the way, follow the river upstream through woods and meadows. As you enter a particularly dark area of woodland, keep close to the water's edge, ignoring the path to the left. ▶

Eventually, you pass a beautifully placed riverside cottage to reach a road leading to a ford. To pick up the continuation of the riverside path, turn right along this road and then immediately left. A stile provides access to a woodland trail continuing with the river on your right.

When you reach the bridge leading to King's Meaburn Mill, do not cross it; instead, cross the rough track and climb the stile behind the barrier (broken at the time of writing). The path is badly eroded after the next stile as walkers have to make their way carefully down a muddy slope where tree roots and slippery rocks have become exposed. Beyond this, though, you're on the riverbank again.

Early summer foliage on the Lyvennet

Jackdaws' Scar, partly hidden by the trees up to your left, is unusual in that it has a layer of exposed limestone on top of a layer of sandstone.

King's Meaburn Mill

After the next stile, the path inches its way along the riverbank very close to the water's edge – something that might present difficulties when water levels are particularly high. After one more stile, keep close to the woods on your left, heading away from the water's edge. As the fence comes to an end, swing slightly left and go through the gate in the hedge straight ahead.

Beyond this, cross the field to a small footbridge. Now head gently uphill, parallel with the fence on the left. Ignore the stile in this fence; instead, cross the stile at the top of the field, about 120m to the left of the farmhouse at **High Whitber**. Turn left along the surfaced lane. Go left along the minor road at **Littlebeck** and then immediately right along a rough track between hedgerows.

Turn right at the T-junction and take the next road on your left towards Colby and Appleby. Savouring the occasional tantalising glimpse of the North Pennines through gaps in the high hedges as you go, walk along this quiet lane for about 1km. When the road bends sharp right, turn left along a wide track beside a house with what must undoubtedly be distracting but enviable views.

The track ends at **Burwain Hall**. Go through the double gate to the right of the large house and walk with the fence on your left. Entering the woods via a large wooden gate, keep straight ahead. The sometimes-muddy path follows the fence on the right at first, but the two quickly separate. Soon after they do so, a faint track is reached. Bear left here to cross the tiny beck, but then immediately swing right to continue in the same direction as before. Keeping just to the left of the trees, you'll have some damp, rough ground to negotiate before you reach a clear track. Turn right along this, quickly following it round to the left.

After the next gate, leave the track by going through another gate straight ahead to access a bridleway between two fences. It may at first look rather overgrown, but the path is easy to follow.

Eventually emerging from the undergrowth, head straight down the track. After passing the farm at **Sockenber**, descend towards a caravan park. Just before the track goes over to asphalt at the site entrance, turn right along a rough track. Go left at a T-junction of tracks and climb to the road. Turn right to walk back to the pub in **King's Meaburn**.

> Both **King's Meaburn** and the nearby village of **Maulds Meaburn** were once in the barony of the 12th-century knight Sir Hugh de Morville, the Lord of Westmorland. He forfeited the land after he and three other knights killed Thomas à Becket, the Archbishop of Canterbury, in 1170. The northern part of the manor reverted to the Crown, and has since been known as King's Meaburn, while the southern part went to Morville's sister Maud, hence Maulds Meaburn.

WALKING IN CUMBRIA'S EDEN VALLEY

WALK 13
Rutter Force and Hoff Beck

Start/finish	St Lawrence's Church, Appleby (NY 683 204)
Distance	7 miles (11.5km)
Total ascent	207m (680ft)
Grade	1–2
Time	3¼hr
Terrain	Farm paths and tracks; some road walking
Maps	OS Explorer OL19 or OS Landranger 91
Transport	Appleby is served by bus 563 and the Settle–Carlisle Railway
Facilities	Pubs, cafés and public toilets in Appleby; New Inn at Hoff

Rutter Force is always an impressive place to visit: dramatic in winter, when river levels are high and a powerful torrent comes raging down the cliff; idyllic in summer when a fine veil of water shrouds one side of the back wall and then flows serenely past the picturesque red sandstone corn mill. This route approaches the waterfall via farm paths and some road walking. Beyond the falls, a lovely beckside path heads back towards Appleby, passing through Hoff along the way. (Time things carefully and you'll hit the hamlet during pub opening hours.) Keep your binoculars handy beside Hoff Beck as there's a good chance of spotting wildlife, including kingfishers, red squirrels and herons. The route holds one final surprise as it climbs away from Hoff Beck and crosses farmland: a magnificent view of the North Pennines, with the distinctive, rock-rimmed valley of High Cup Gill (Walk 14) cutting deep into the escarpment.

With your back to St Lawrence's Church, walk straight up Boroughgate, the main road through the centre of **Appleby**. On reaching the entrance to the castle, follow the road round to the right. Take the road on the right signposted to Colby – not the road that seems to head back down towards the town centre.

After about 130m, as the road swings slightly right, take the path signposted to Bandley Bridge on the left. This goes through a normally open gate and over a stile. Head up the left-hand edge of the field. After the stile in the top corner, turn right and then, almost immediately, cross the small, metal ladder stile on the left. Head uphill again with the field boundary.

Leaving the field at the next stile, turn left along the broad track. Turn right at the **B6260** and follow it through **Burrells**. On the far side of the village, soon after Friendship Farm, take the bridle track signposted to Lookingflatt on the left. Once through the gate, the track leads across a field. When it swings right, go through the gate on the bend to continue in exactly the same direction as before. ▸

Beyond the gate at the far end, you briefly join an enclosed track. After the next gate, head downhill with the field boundary on your left. Go through a gate at the bottom of the slope and then head towards the farm buildings at **Lookingflatt**. Unfortunately, there are no fingerposts or waymarkers to guide you here.

Go through a gate to enter the farmyard. Turn left along the access lane, but only for a few strides. As soon as you pass the last building, head up to the right to locate a gate next to a shed. Go through this and keep to the right-hand edge of the field. After the next gate, continue in exactly the same direction to reach a minor road.

This long, narrow field affords good views of the North Pennines to the east.

WALKING IN CUMBRIA'S EDEN VALLEY

Rutter Force and the mill

Turn right and, having walked the lane for about 650m, take the turning for the waterfall on the right.

Just before you reach the ford, a trail on the left leads to the footbridge across **Hoff Beck** and its great view of **Rutter Force**.

Rutter Mill, beside the waterfall, has served many purposes during its long lifetime. It has been a corn mill, a bobbin mill and a timber mill. From 1928 until 1951 it was even used to generate electricity – albeit an unreliable supply – for homes in and around Great Asby.

Having crossed the footbridge, head up the lane and, almost immediately, go through a gap in the hedgerows and trees on the right to join a footpath signposted to Hoff. In the summer, the first few hundred metres of this path are swamped by wildflowers and other riverside vegetation, but you'll quickly reach a stile beyond which the walking is easy.

Head downstream along the riverbank as far as a footbridge. Cross **Hoff Beck** here and continue downstream

WALK 13 – RUTTER FORCE AND HOFF BECK

– with the water now on your left. Keep close to the riverbank, crossing several stiles as you make your way from one field to the next. Ignore a vehicle-wide bridge over the beck; simply cross the track here to continue on your beckside journey. It's not long before you reach another bridge – this time a footbridge. Use this to cross back to the west bank. (The steps up to it on the east bank were damaged at the time of writing, but the bridge itself was open.)

Make for a gate to the right. Beyond this, follow the rough track to a quiet lane, along which you turn right. Cross straight over the **B6260** in **Hoff**.

Follow the stony track – signposted Bandley Bridge. In a few metres, the lane splits. Pass between the large white house on the right and a red-stone cottage called Stonekirk. Go through a metal gate and veer right through another gate, to regain the riverbank. Keep close to the beck as you pass through the first few fields. Then, as you cross a stile followed immediately by a kissing-gate, go through another gate on the left to enter a large field. Keep close to the fence on the right to continue downstream. On the far side of the field, go through another small gate. Cross the stile next to the large gate here to join a lovely path right beside the beck.

Soon after climbing some steps, cross a stile and follow a trail downhill through the trees. The next gate leads into a riverside field. Drop diagonally right to a gate that provides access to Bandley Bridge. Cross this and bear left, through a gate, to enter Rachel's Wood. Keep right on a faint trail through the long vegetation, staying close to the boundary wall on the right. Just a few strides into this area of young woodland, go through a small (and easy-to-miss) gated stile on the right.

Head half-left up the field, aiming for a single tree close to a fence corner. Veer slightly right – with the fence – to reach a gate and stile.

You can see Appleby Castle's Norman keep straight ahead now, but even more impressive is the scene behind it – the distinctive, U-shaped valley of High Cup Gill slicing deep into the Pennine escarpment.

Looking towards High Cup

Cross the stile and veer slightly right of your previous line. After the next stile, turn left to walk beside the field boundary. The next stile leads to a track between hedgerows. Turn right along this and, after about 175m, cross the stile next to the gate on your left to enter a field.

Retracing your steps from earlier in the walk, head downhill beside the field boundary. Remember to bear right after the next stile and then continue down the right-hand side of the ensuing field to reach Colby Lane. Turn right and then left at the main road to return to the town centre.

WALK 14
High Cup and Scordale

Start/finish	Car park on northeast edge of Murton, near Appleby (NY 729 220). If approaching Murton from the south, turn right along the dead-end lane just before leaving the village. There is a gated car park at the far end of the lane
Distance	13¾ miles (22km)
Total ascent	627m (2057ft)
Grade	5
Time	8hr
Terrain	Road at start; good tracks; rough, boggy, pathless moorland
Maps	OS Explorer OL19 or OS Landranger 91
Transport	None
Facilities	Pubs, cafés and public toilets in nearby Appleby or Dufton

A chance to explore two of the most dramatic and interesting valleys in the North Pennines: one well known and much loved, the other rarely visited because of restricted access. The first is High Cup, one of the most famous sights in the Pennines, a line of exposed whin sill rock that forms a spectacular rim around a broad, U-shaped valley. The next is Scordale, a narrower valley where limestone dominates and few walkers venture because it's on Ministry of Defence (MoD) land. The two are linked by following bridleways across high, open moorland – easy at first where the route coincides with the Pennine Way, but rough underfoot and with few obvious paths as it parts company with the long-distance route. The route involves a ford that could be tricky after heavy rain.

About 13km into the walk, the Warcop Training Area is entered. Access to this area is restricted to non-live firing times. Firing stops at 1pm every Sunday, making this walk possible on non-winter Sundays. There are also several weekends when there is no firing. For updates on accessibility, phone 0800 7835 181 or visit www.gov.uk/government/publications/warcop-access-times.

WALKING IN CUMBRIA'S EDEN VALLEY

From the car park, walk back down the lane you just drove up and then turn right at the crossroads – towards Dufton. Having walked this road for about 3.2km, turn right along a rough track – signposted High Cup Nick via Bow Hall.

As the track bends right, go through the gate on the left. Walk straight across the field to a kissing-gate in the wall opposite. Once through this, swing up to the right to go through a gate in the top wall. Now turn left to walk

WALK 14 – HIGH CUP AND SCORDALE

beside the wall, quickly passing the buildings of High Cup Winery.

Skirting the base of the fells, keep the wall on your left, passing through several gates along the way. After one of several small bridges, you're faced with a choice of two gates: go through the left-hand one to walk with a wall on your right.

On reaching a track just above **Bow Hall**, turn right – signposted High Cup Gill. This is the Pennine Way, which is followed for several kilometres. After a gate, the walls enclosing the bridleway are lost, but the track continues steadily uphill. Beyond the next set of gates,

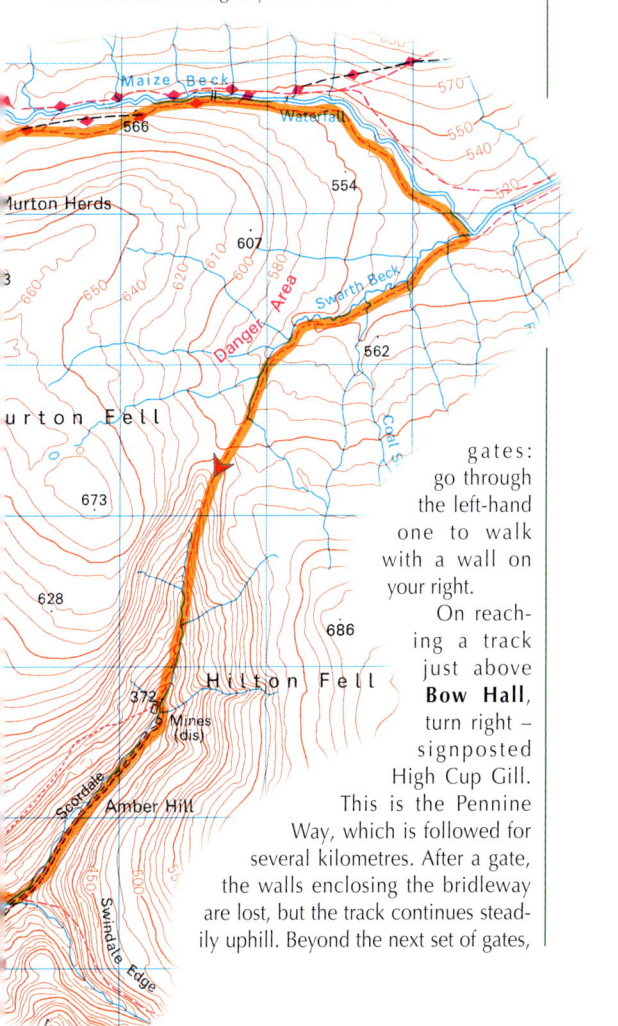

WALKING IN CUMBRIA'S EDEN VALLEY

Walking the northern rim of High Cup Gill

the way ahead is less obvious. Head straight up a grassy gap between rocky outcrops. After about 140m, veer left at a cairn to climb to a cairn on the brow of the slope ahead. The path now becomes clearer again.

Eventually, you'll catch your first glimpse of the rock columns on the south side of **High Cup Gill**. With every step taken, the scale of this amazing natural feature becomes more apparent and yet, at the same time, harder to grasp.

DOLERITE

The huge columns forming the rim around High Cup Gill are made of dolerite, a volcanic rock formed within the earth. This was created towards the end of the Carboniferous period when movement of tectonic plates forced magma to be squeezed sideways between beds of existing rock. The magma, as it then slowly cooled, crystallised and shrank, forming hexagonal columns. With dolerite being resistant to erosion, it forms striking landscape features such as here at High Cup, but also at High Force where the River Tees crosses the line of volcanic rock to form one of England's most impressive waterfalls.

This layer of dolerite is known as the Great Whin Sill and forms a line through the North Pennines and Northumberland as far as Lindisfarne.

WALK 14 – HIGH CUP AND SCORDALE

> Several castles and much of Hadrian's Wall are built on top of the Great Whin Sill, the resulting cliffs forming an extra line of defence against attack.
>
> One of the most famous examples of dolerite in the UK can be found in Edinburgh – on Salisbury Crags near Arthur's Seat. It was here in the late 18th century that James Hutton, known as the father of modern geology, found the evidence to help him explain the relationships between different rock types. He used the dolerite here, now known as Hutton's Section, as part of his fundamental theories on how the earth formed over very long periods of geological time and was still forming today.

The route is straightforward, but there is a split as you reach an area of landslips and the first of several squat stone markers. As indicated by the arrow, the Pennine Way heads left – the more vertiginous, right-hand route having to negotiate some rough ground. Take either. After the two reunite, head out along the grassy top of the northern side of the dale. Keep to this edge until you reach **High Cup Nick**, the point at which a shallow beck drops into the valley. Having forded this trickle, swing left (northeast) towards another stone marker. Keep to this broad path, ignoring less obvious paths to the right.

Striding out easily across the open, grassy moorland, you'll soon see **Maize Beck** down to the left. Our route parts company with the Pennine Way at the next bridge. As the long-distance route crosses over, keep to the south side of the beck. There's a faint path at first, but this disappears and you're left to make your own way downstream on sometimes rough, sometimes damp ground. Signs warn of entry on to the Warcop range.

> **The Warcop Training Area**, established in 1942 as a tank gunnery range, covers more than 9700 hectares in the North Pennines. Most of the armoured formations which took part in the D-Day landings at the end of World War Two trained here. Today, it is largely used as an infantry field firing range, but also caters for tank-mounted guns and other armoured vehicles.

About two-thirds of the range falls within a Site of Special Scientific Interest, protected for its blanket bog, limestone pavements, calcareous grassland and alpine and sub-alpine plants.

At 788m (2585ft), Mickle Fell used to be the highest point in Yorkshire. After the local government reorganisation of 1974, and the shifting of county borders, it became the highest point in County Durham.

After toiling for about 1.9km beyond the bridge over Maize Beck, and with Mickle Fell looming to the south-east, you reach the **Swarth Beck** confluence. ◄

Carefully ford Swarth Beck and, waving goodbye to Maize Beck, turn right. Swarth Beck now acts as your guide as you make your way upstream. Rather surprisingly, there is a faint trail at times, making life easier, but it disappears occasionally. Follow the beck for 2.1km, passing some of the UK's highest limestone formations. When the beck finally peters out, continue south-southwest over Swarth Beck Head. Pass to the right of a rocky mound to reach a waymarker post at Scordale Head – and a view of the fells to the west.

Work your way south-southwest through the peat hags and then head downhill, aiming for the top end of the valley. Drop over a limestone lip to enter the valley proper. The first section of **Scordale** is narrow and steep-sided – an exciting but confined descent. There's no beck

Limestone crags in Scordale

until the dale opens out and a torrent comes thundering down from the right. A few hundred metres after this, cross to the western side of the valley. Don't be tempted by the trail upslope to a metal post; simply continue south, down through the valley. Eventually, you'll pick up a line of waymarker posts that drop to old mine workings. Leats hugging the hillside will try to lure you away from your descent, but these should be resisted; continue downhill until you reach an old track in the valley bottom.

> **Lead** had been mined in Scordale for several centuries before the London Lead Company came along in 1824 and started mining on an industrial scale. Towards the end of the 19th century, as British firms struggled to compete with cheap imports particularly from Spain and the USA, the extraction of lead ceased, but barytes continued to be mined. This mineral was used in the production of paints, plastics and armaments. Operations in the valley finally ended in 1939.

The track now makes for easy walking, although one section of it has been inundated by **Scordale Beck**. Cross the beck via a substantial footbridge – about 1.6km after joining the track. Veer right, along the top of the embankment, briefly heading back upstream to reach a stile. Cross this and climb straight up the slope. After about 60m, a faint trail is reached. Turn left along this. It widens as it joins another path from the right.

The clear route leads to a gate. Cross the stile a few metres to the right of it. The right-of-way now heads west-northwest, sometimes on the clear path, sometimes on pathless ground. Beyond the next stile, it passes just above an unusual depression. Continuing west-northwest, you'll eventually reach a stony track. Turn left along this. Having forded Murton Beck, cross the stile next to the gate. After a few more metres on the rough track, go through the kissing-gate on the left to re-enter the car park where the walk began.

WALKING IN CUMBRIA'S EDEN VALLEY

WALK 15
Murton Pike

Start/finish	Car park on northeast edge of Murton, near Appleby (NY 729 220). If you're approaching Murton from the south, turn right along the dead-end lane just before leaving the village. There is a gated car park at the far end of the lane
Distance	4 miles (6.5km)
Total ascent	378m (1240ft)
Grade	2–3
Time	2¾hr
Terrain	Open fell, pathless and damp in places
Maps	OS Explorer OL19 or OS Landranger 91
Transport	None
Facilities	Pubs, cafés and public toilets in nearby Appleby or Dufton

Murton Pike is a conical peak that towers over the tiny fellside village of Murton at the base of the North Pennines. A great vantage point, with views across the Eden Valley to the Lake District fells, it reaches the respectable height of 594m (1948ft). By approaching the fell in a roundabout way via Trundale Gill, this walk also samples the remote moorland to the north and east.

From the car park, go through the gate on to the access land at the base of the open fells. You'll see two tracks here: the one to the right often has a red flag flying, indicating that the Ministry of Defence's Warcop firing ranges are in use. Our route uses the track to the left. Although we don't head into the area of live firing, Murton Pike is within the Ministry of Defence's 'Area Victor' where there's still a chance of encountering military personnel.

After just 140m, leave the stony track by bearing left along a grassy track that sticks to the base of **Murton Pike**. As the track swings slightly left, it splits. Take either

WALK 15 – MURTON PIKE

option here; they reunite just before crossing a small beck issuing from Trough Keld spring.

You're soon able to look across the Eden Valley to the left – towards the eastern Lake District fells, including High Street.

As the wall on your left becomes a fence and the track narrows, if you're on the lower path, you want to think about getting on to the higher path, which is about 50m up from the wall/fence. This becomes essential as the fence swings slightly left and the ground beside it becomes damp and rushy.

Having negotiated the steep ground along the western base of Murton Pike, you will see a fence immediately ahead. Bear right, joining a reasonably clear path running beside the fence. This gradually makes its way up into Trundale Gill.

Before long, you're walking with the beck on your immediate left. The slopes on either side have eased back slightly, although there are some limestone crags up to the right.

The red flag indicates live firing on the Warcop range

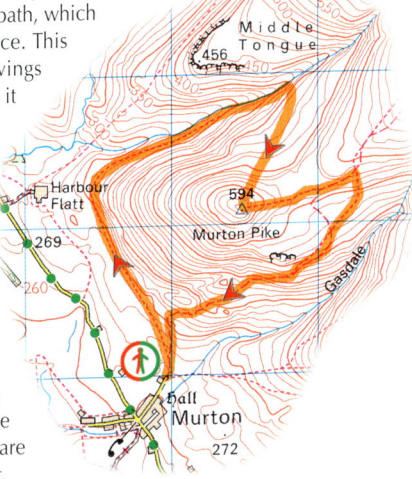

105

WALKING IN CUMBRIA'S EDEN VALLEY

After passing a waymarker post, the valley constricts considerably. Second and third posts keep you on the straight and narrow as you continue on the south side of the beck. The trail is narrow in places and, due to the underlying limestone, can get slippery in wet weather. If you followed this little side valley to its conclusion, you'd eventually come out on the damp, windswept top of Murton Fell – 673m above sea level. Looking higher into the confines of this secluded ravine, it's tempting to continue, but we leave it long before we get that high.

About 180m beyond the third waymarker, watch for a post up on the hillside to the right. Climb directly to this: the slope is steep and there's no path, but the distance is short.

The neat little, bomb crater-like holes that pockmark the landscape aren't the result of military activity; they are shake holes, naturally formed by the interaction of water and limestone.

On reaching the post, you'll see the top of Murton Pike to the southwest. Make directly for this, following a line of waymarker posts across the bleak moorland – damp and rough underfoot. ◄

The gradient suddenly increases as you reach the northern slopes of Murton Pike. Follow the waymarker posts to the trig pillar. The views suddenly open out, taking in the Lake District to the west and the Howgills and Wild Boar Fell to the south.

To descend, head east and you'll quickly pick up a trail heading steeply downhill. On reaching a stony track, turn right. With **Gasdale** down to the left, this track allows for an easy saunter all the way back to **Murton**. It winds its way around the southern flanks of Murton Pike, cutting beneath the limestone cliff of Murton Crag and eventually reaching the car park where the walk began.

The return track winds its way around the southern flanks of Murton Pike

WALK 16
Flakebridge Wood and Dufton Ghyll

Start/finish	Car park in Dufton (NY 689 249)
Distance	6 miles (9.5km)
Total ascent	247m (810ft)
Grade	1–2
Time	3hr
Terrain	Farmland; tracks; quiet roads; woodland paths
Maps	OS Explorer OL19 or OS Landranger 91
Transport	None
Facilities	The Stag Inn and Post Box Pantry, Dufton; public toilets in car park

Strolling across farmland, through woods and alongside becks at the base of the Pennines near Dufton makes for a wonderful day out at any time of the year, but this walk is at its very best during bluebell season. Flakebridge Wood is one of the best places in Cumbria to view these beautiful flowers, forming a carpet of blue as far as the eye can see. Dufton Ghyll, too, is a gorgeous location, full of colour in the spring as winter aconite, wood anemones, bluebells and pignut burst into flower.

Leaving the car park in **Dufton**, turn right along the road and immediately right again, along a track between the campsite and car park. This drops into Dufton Ghyll. As it swings right, turn left along a narrow path and cross the footbridge. Once over the beck, turn left to follow it upstream through the gorgeous gill – beside moss-covered cliffs at first.

Turn left at the road and then immediately right over a stile. Follow the tiny beck on your right and, just after crossing it, climb the stile to access a farm track. Head straight towards a large cattle shed at **Greenhow** and through a gate, passing to the left of the building on a concrete track.

WALKING IN CUMBRIA'S EDEN VALLEY

Dufton Ghyll

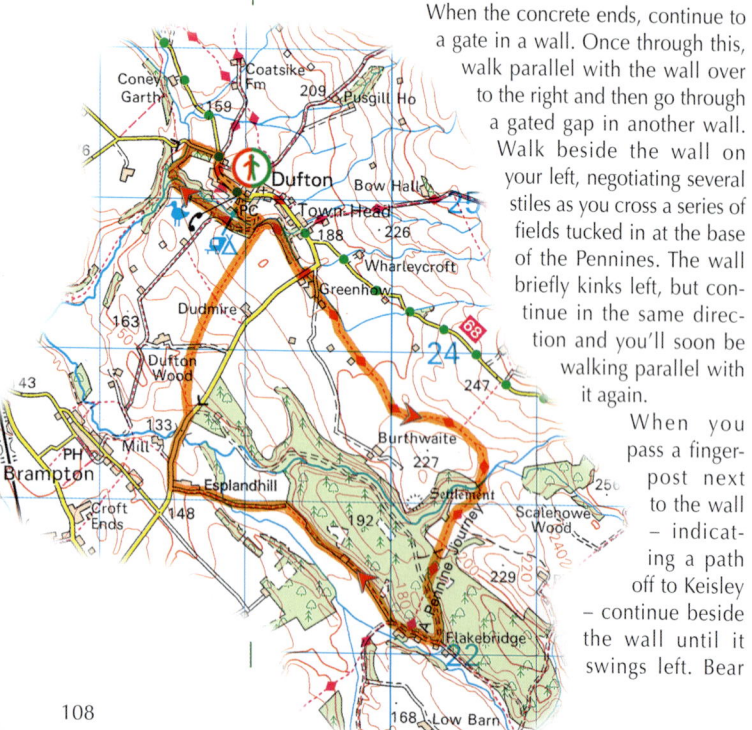

When the concrete ends, continue to a gate in a wall. Once through this, walk parallel with the wall over to the right and then go through a gated gap in another wall. Walk beside the wall on your left, negotiating several stiles as you cross a series of fields tucked in at the base of the Pennines. The wall briefly kinks left, but continue in the same direction and you'll soon be walking parallel with it again.

When you pass a fingerpost next to the wall – indicating a path off to Keisley – continue beside the wall until it swings left. Bear

108

Walk 16 – Flakebridge Wood and Dufton Ghyll

right here, along the base of a slope on the right. Once over the Keisley Beck footbridge, cross the stile to the left and then bear right to pick up the line of a wall for a short while. When this wall swings away to the right, swing slightly left of your previous line to cross a stile in a wall at the top of the field. With views that take in Wild Boar Fell, the Howgills and the Lake District's eastern fells, keep to the same line. Beyond the next stile, bear half-left to drop to cross a ladder stile in the field corner.

Entering **Flakebridge Wood**, a narrow path swings right and crosses a bridge to join a track along which you turn right. At a crossing of ways, go straight over, heading gently uphill through the woods. ▶ As you approach a fenced compound, turn right, following a narrow, way-marked trail.

In spring these woods are full of bluebells.

The UK is now home to several different types of **bluebell**. The ones you see in woods, hedges and other shady places tend to be the familiar native bluebell, known as wild hyacinth in Scotland. The Spanish bluebell was introduced to gardens many years ago and is sometimes now also found in the

Bluebells in Flakebridge Wood

countryside. A hybrid, which is seen as a potential threat to the native plant, is now more common than its Spanish parent.

Turn right on reaching a track near the edge of the woods and then keep right – signposted Esplandhill. Keep close to the fence – briefly a wall – on your left until you reach a stile. Cross this and continue with the woodland boundary on your right.

Go through a gate providing access to a grassy track known as Frith Lane. This passes the farm at **Esplandhill** to reach a road. Turn right and walk along the asphalt for 500m. You'll pass and ignore two signposted public rights-of-way to the left early on. The third takes the form of a rough track rising beyond a gate on the left about 100m after the road crosses Stock Bridge. Take this. When it emerges in a field, walk beside the wall on your right.

Beyond a gate, the route drops to a farm track. Cross straight over and go through the wooden gate into a field. Without a path to guide you, head north-northeast up the slope and then down into the far left-hand corner of the field. Climb the old stone steps here and over the wall, ignoring the path to the left. Head up the field with the wall on your right.

A wall stile provides access to delightful Dufton Ghyll, home to bluebells, pignut, angelica and wood anemone in the spring. Drop on to the main path through the top part of the woods and turn left. Go straight over at two route crossings, staying on the higher path with views down into the impressive gorge. This eventually drops to cross a bridge. Keep to the main path, soon following Mill Beck upstream.

This **woodland** is classed as semi-natural ancient woodland. Managed by The Woodland Trust, the charity began to replant native species such as oak, rowan and ash in the 1980s. The woods contain several disused quarries from which St Bees sandstone was once extracted.

WALK 16 – FLAKEBRIDGE WOOD AND DUFTON GHYLL

Crossing farmland tucked in at the foot of the Pennines

Turn right at the road and right again at a T-junction – signposted Appleby and Dufton. Follow the road round to the left. The car park where the walk started is on the right soon after the village green.

WALK 17
Dufton Pike

Start/finish	Car park in Dufton (NY 689 249)
Distance	4 miles (6.5km)
Total ascent	326m (1070ft)
Grade	2–3
Time	2¾hr
Terrain	Farmland; grassy ridge path; tracks
Maps	OS Explorer OL19 or OS Landranger 91
Transport	None
Facilities	The Stag Inn and Post Box Pantry, Dufton; public toilets in car park

Just like its neighbour Murton Pike to the southeast, Dufton Pike seems to tower over its eponymous village. But at just 481m (1578ft) its 'towering' nature is an illusion, and its ridges are nowhere near as steep as they appear from Dufton. A walk along the full length of the pike's mostly grassy spine makes for a lovely and relatively straightforward excursion.

Leaving the car park, turn left and walk along the main road through **Dufton**.

> The pretty red sandstone village of **Dufton**, which is built around a long green and an avenue of lime trees, has a hall and cottages dating back to the 16th and 17th centuries. During the 18th century the Quaker-owned London Lead Company took control of lead mining in the area and soon began building cottages for its workers and their families in the village. They also provided Dufton with a school, a library and piped water.

Having left the village and passed a turning on the left, the road bends left. Leave it here by turning right,

WALK 17 – DUFTON PIKE

along a wide track towards **Coatsyke Farm** (Coatsike Fm on map extract). This is known as Hurning Lane and it soon joins the Pennine Way.

As you go through the farmyard, keep to the left of the main group of buildings. Continue along the muddy track with the field boundary on your left. You leave the confines of the tree-lined lane when you reach the abandoned farmhouse at Halsteads. The more open track now climbs gently on to Cosca Hill where you get a good view across to Knock Pike.

The track then drops to a gate beside **Great Rundale Beck**. Don't go through this; instead, continue on the southern side of the stream, along a gently rising track. This

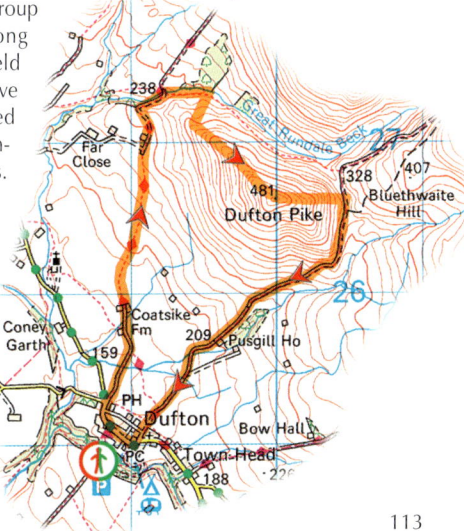

Dufton

WALKING IN CUMBRIA'S EDEN VALLEY

hidden valley sees little sun in the winter, but it is a lovely spot in the spring and summer when the leaves and blossom return to its stunted trees, which include hazel and hawthorn.

The track briefly becomes indistinct after a gate: simply continue in the same direction across the open hillside. After going through a small, gated stile in a wall, you'll see a fenced area of saplings on the right. Continue on the track for now, but then, at the far end of the fenced area, turn sharp right along a narrow trail climbing beside the fence. The trail quickly hits another grassy track, along which you turn right.

After a few hundred metres, you reach a point where you can see across the Eden Valley and to the Lake District beyond. Now turn left to head straight up Dufton Pike's grassy ridge. The route steepens as you approach the top, but before you know it, the hard work is over and you are rewarded with the sight of hills in all directions. The Lake District has been visible since joining the ridge, but it's now joined by some of its neighbours. Looking down the line of the Pennine chain, Murton Pike stands out as another conical top sitting at the base of the higher fells. ◂

To the south are Wild Boar Fell and the Howgills, and Cross Fell looms to the north.

Dufton Pike

WALK 17 – DUFTON PIKE

A reasonably clear path continues down the other side of the ridge. Keep to the clearest route at all times. It eventually plummets to a kissing-gate, beyond which you turn right along a clear track.

Reaching the edge of **Dufton**, bear right along the road. It soon swings right and, just after it does so, you'll see the car park on your left.

Looking into Great Rundale from the top of Dufton Pike

WALK 18
High Cup via Great Rundale

Start/finish	Car park in Dufton (NY 689 249)
Distance	10 miles (16km)
Total ascent	674m (2210ft)
Grade	4
Time	5½hr
Terrain	Good tracks and boggy, pathless moorland
Maps	OS Explorer OL19 or OS Landranger 91
Transport	None
Facilities	The Stag Inn and Post Box Pantry, Dufton; public toilets in car park

Our second visit to High Cup approaches it from the north – the aficionado's route. It heads up into the once heavily mined valley of Great Rundale before striking out across the bleak but beautiful moorland to the southeast of Great Rundale Tarn. The paths up here are faint at best, but the tarn's outlet stream, which becomes Maize Beck, acts as a reliable guide for much of the way. Any difficulties are then rewarded as High Cup is revealed – its magnificence greatly enhanced by the suddenness of its appearance.

Leaving the car park in **Dufton**, turn right and follow the road as it bends left. When it then bends right, walk up the lane between the sandstone buildings straight ahead. Having ignored the track that bears left around the back of the buildings, stride out down the pleasant lane, soon passing the turning for the Pennine Way on your left. Eventually, you leave farmland behind as you reach a pair of gates providing access to more open country at the foot of **Dufton Pike**. Before long, the pleasant, rolling landscape formed by the Pennine foothills is replaced by a more rugged aspect as the track heads up into **Great Rundale**, enclosed by steep rock walls and the remains of old mine workings. ◀

Lead was mined in Great Rundale from the 18th century until about 1900 followed by barytes extraction until the mid 1920s. The dumps were also worked for a while in the 1980s.

WALK 18 – HIGH CUP VIA GREAT RUNDALE

Despite what it says on some maps, the track continues all the way to the 'shooting box' on the moors proper. This, at 678m (2224ft), is the highest point on the walk. Immediately after the shooting box, turn right along a stream bed to reach **Great Rundale Tarn**. Bearing left at the water's edge, walk around the side of this peaceful, peaty pool until you reach its outlet stream, ignoring a tempting vehicle-wide track heading off to the left.

This outlet stream is the key to the next section of the walk, which crosses wild, remote Pennine moorland. You must follow it for the next 2.2km, until you reach Maizebeck Bridge. The best way to begin is to cross the outlet stream at the tarn and follow a narrow, but fairly solid path downstream for a while, but whichever side you choose you end up criss-crossing the main channel for the first 800m or so. There are faint paths on the ground at times, especially where there are grouse butts nearby, but what is a fairly straightforward stroll in a dry summer or hard frost becomes a soggy, peaty mess in wet weather. After the first 800m the best option is to keep to the northeast side of the beck.

Eventually, you reach **Maizebeck Bridge**, which crosses the deep dark gorge below. Once over, make for

Great Rundale Tarn

WALKING IN CUMBRIA'S EDEN VALLEY

High Cup Gill

the stone pillar just 10m ahead and then bear left (south-southwest) along a faint path. Take care here because the path is not always clear. Your bearing becomes more southwesterly as you head across the flat expanse of **High Cup Plain**. You will know when you have arrived at **High Cup** itself: the ground ahead suddenly drops away and you are greeted by its truly breath-taking dimensions. Enormous columns of dolerite rock form a rim around the huge glaciated valley of High Cup Gill.

Turn right along a clear, grassy path a few metres back from the edge. In 450m, just before the main path starts to rise, bear left to follow an interesting path that sticks to a wide, natural ledge with steep drops to the left. Having carefully forded a shallow but slippery beck, either continue along this rough ledge path or use the slightly better path a few metres back from

WALK 18 – HIGH CUP VIA GREAT RUNDALE

the edge. Before long they join up, and eventually you make your way down through limestone outcrops and shake-holes to a gate. Once over the stile beside it, stride out along the clear track heading gently downhill with lovely views across to the Lake District.

There is a slight sense of disappointment when the rough track turns to asphalt and you know that your long day on the fells is coming to an end. Turn right at a T-junction and follow the road back into **Dufton**. The car park is on the left just before you reach the village green.

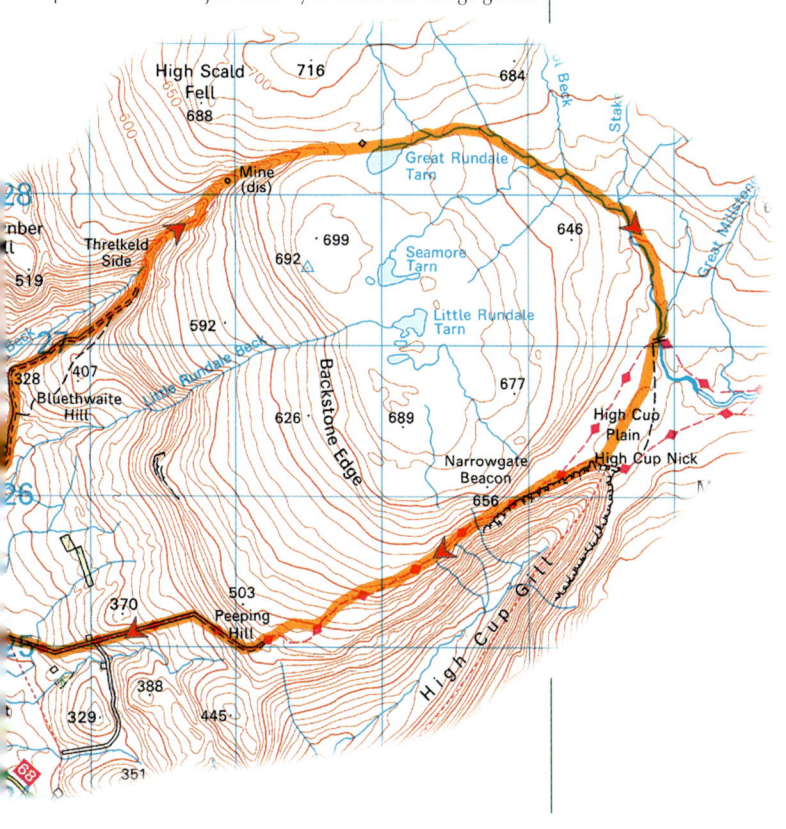

Walking in Cumbria's Eden Valley

WALK 19
Cross Fell

Start/finish	Parish Council noticeboards and recycling point in Blencarn (NY 638 312). Please park considerately nearby in the village
Distance	10¼ miles (16.5km)
Total ascent	762m (2500ft)
Grade	4
Time	5¾hr
Terrain	Good paths and tracks on open moorland, wet in places
Maps	OS Explorer OL31 or OS Landranger 91
Transport	None
Facilities	Nearest pubs and cafés are in Langwathby, Kirkby Thore, Temple Sowerby and Culgaith

No guide to the Eden Valley would be complete without an ascent of the fell that seems to loom over much of this area. At 893m (2929ft), Cross Fell is the highest point along the entire Pennine chain, and it dominates the view on many of the walks in this book. There are several ways to reach this wild, windswept top, and none of them is short; this route from Blencarn is probably the shortest and most straightforward of them. It ascends a mostly clear, grassy bridleway that gradually climbs all the way to the source of the River Tees. From here, it joins the Pennine Way to cross the large flat summit with its expansive views. The descent is via another mostly clear track.

With your back to the Parish Council noticeboards in **Blencarn**, turn left and, when the road bends right, keep straight ahead towards a gate. Go through this and swing left along the rough track. Ignoring another track off to the right early on, this strip of access land, contained within two drystone walls, soon begins to narrow. The track ends close to a small farm shed, but you

WALK 19 – CROSS FELL

Wythwaite lies at the foot of the Pennines

should continue along the narrowing strip. The path mostly keeps close to the wall on the right, but patches of gorse force it to deviate from this line from time to time.

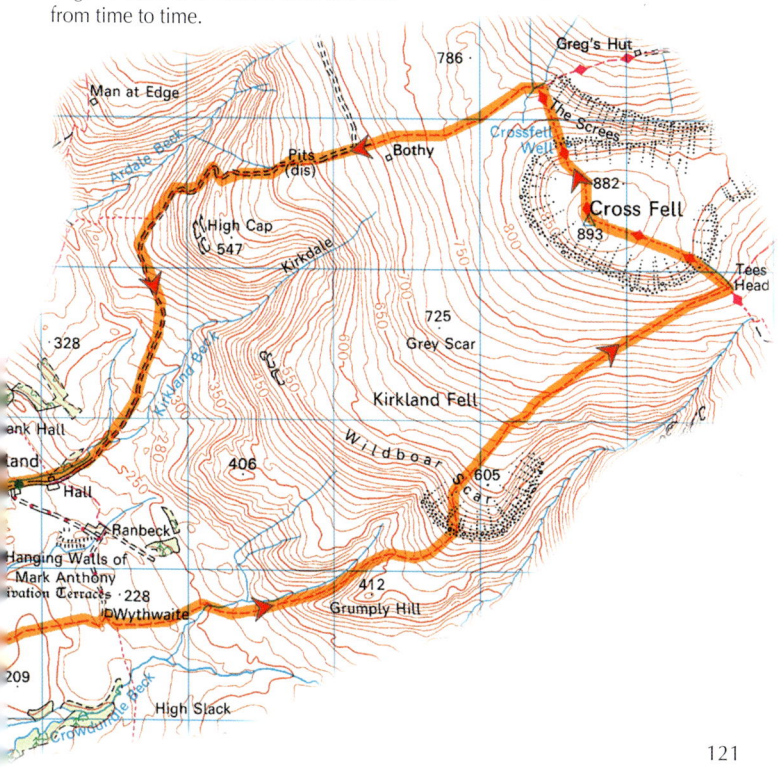

WALKING IN CUMBRIA'S EDEN VALLEY

About 500m after passing the public byway off to the left near the house at **Wythwaite**, go through two gates in quick succession to access open land at the base of the fells. Using a wide, grassy path, keep close to Littledale Beck on your right. Having ignored a narrow trail to the left, quickly ford the beck and then continue upstream.

There are two hills either side of the beck – **Grumply Hill** to the south and **Moray Hill** to the north. Aim for the base of Grumply Hill, ignoring a track heading left on to Moray Hill. At the base of Grumply Hill, don't be tempted by the path uphill to the right; simply keep following the clear, grassy bridleway as it heads further up into the valley.

The ascent is reasonably steady at first, but then becomes steeper as the bridleway suddenly does a left turn to climb across the front of **Wildboar Scar**. As it swings right again, keep to the clearest path that winds its way up through an area littered with piles of stones. The gradient then eases considerably and you get a good view of Little Dun and Great Dun fells. ◄

> The golfball-like contraption on Great Dun Fell is part of the Civil Aviation Authority's air traffic control radar.

The ground can be soggy in places as you approach Tees Head and it is easy to lose the path temporarily in the quagmire. There are, however, cairns to guide you as you head east-northeast. When you reach the paved ridge path – the route of the Pennine Way – turn left. ◄

> This area of the Pennines is known for its Arctic/Alpine plants, such as the spring gentian. They colonised the area after the last glacial period and have survived ever since.

This is the **English watershed**; all becks flowing west of this ridge end up in the Irish Sea and everything to the east goes to the North Sea. One of the great rivers of the North, the Tees, has its source here. It plummets down through the Pennines via the waterfalls at Cauldron Snout and High Force, meanders its way through County Durham and reaches the sea just beyond Stockton and Middlesbrough, about 85 miles from where it started.

As the flagstones end, keep heading straight up the slope, and eventually you will reach the first in a line of tall cairns that guide you west-northwest across the substantial summit plateau. The top of **Cross Fell** is marked

On Cross Fell

by a trig pillar and a large, cross-shaped shelter that was restored in 2014. ▶

From the shelter follow the cairned path – north at first and then veering northwest. As you drop down the northern side of the fell, pass to the right of **Crossfell Well**, beyond which the going gets decidedly soggy. It is hard to make out the path here, but as long as you head roughly north-northwest you will eventually return to dry land as you reach a wide, clear track.

> This track was once a '**corpse road**'. Before the churchyard in Garrigill was consecrated, villagers used to have to carry their dead over the Pennines to Kirkland for burial at St Lawrence's Church. Corpse roads used to be a common occurrence in Cumbria, and there are famous examples between Wasdale and Eskdale, near Grasmere, and at Loweswater. They frequently crossed bleak and lonely fells and, inevitably, are often associated with ghost stories.

As befits the highest point along 'England's backbone', the view is magnificent: a long line of Lake District fells, the Cheviots and the hills of Dumfries and Galloway are all visible.

Turn left and the long descent to Kirkland soon begins with some great views across the patchwork of fields that make up the Eden Valley to the Lake District beyond. The track can best be described as intermittent in its early stages. Its general direction is west-southwest until it reaches some disused **mine workings**. Then it becomes a lot clearer as it begins to wind its way downhill.

Having gone through several gates and passed **Kirkland Hall**, the track becomes a surfaced lane. At the junction close to the church in Kirkland, keep straight ahead towards Blencarn. About 500m beyond the junction, go through the stile next to a gate on your left. The right-of-way cuts diagonally across this field (south). As you approach a tiny patch of woodland, keep to the top of a small ridge of land, with the fence on your left. Go through a small gate and follow the narrow trail through the trees and over a stile. Walk with the fence on your left and then, immediately after a footbridge, cross the stile on your left. Continue in the same direction as before, but this time with the fence on your right.

Follow the fence round to the left and then, when you reach a wall, go through the gate on the right. When the fence over to your right kinks right, make your way over to it and follow it until you reach a gate. Don't go through this; instead, turn sharp left and walk uphill to another gate. Once through this, walk with the fence on your right and then go through the gate in the field corner on the edge of **Blencarn**. Follow the gravel track to the road and turn left to return to where the walk started.

WALK 20

Long Meg and Her Daughters

Start/finish	Little Salkeld Watermill (NY 566 360). Please don't leave your car at the watermill itself, which has only a small parking area. If you're coming from the Langwathby direction, continue uphill past the watermill and then, when the road bends right, turn left. Park nearby.
Distance	4¾ miles (7.5km)
Total ascent	138m (452ft)
Grade	1
Time	2hr
Terrain	Quiet roads; good tracks; field paths
Maps	OS Explorer OL5 or OS Landrangers 90 and 91
Transport	None
Facilities	Little Salkeld Watermill's tearoom

You should allow plenty of time for sightseeing and general dawdling on this sublime walk through some of the Eden Valley's prettiest countryside. The gentle route visits a water-powered corn mill that is also home to a lovely little café, a lonely church that has lost its village, and, probably the highlight of the excursion, one of the most impressive and most mysterious stone circles in Britain.

With your back to the watermill in **Little Salkeld**, turn right along the road and then follow it round to the right, towards Glassonby and Gamblesby. Having walked about 600m from the watermill – and with views across to the highest of the Pennines opening out to your right – turn left on a rough track. Follow it round to the right and then, on reaching a surfaced lane, keep straight on. Before too long, you'll reach the stone circle known as **Long Meg and Her Daughters**. Take some time to explore this large and fascinating site. Long Meg herself is up to the left, standing separate from the main circle.

LONG MEG AND HER DAUGHTERS

This is probably one of the most enigmatic sites in the whole of Cumbria. This huge stone circle, which has a road running through it, consists of 59 stones, although originally there were about 70. The largest stone is Long Meg herself, a 3.6m-tall standing stone that bears faint traces of mysterious cup and ring markings as well as concentric circles, which are thought to be 4500 years old. Constructed of red sandstone quarried from the banks of the River Eden, she is positioned just outside the circle. Seen from the centre of the circle, she is aligned with the midwinter sunset.

Needless to say, there are a lot of spooky local legends associated with this atmospheric site. The stones are said to be the petrified remains of a coven of witches who were turned to stone by Scottish wizard Michael Scot for profanities on the Sabbath. The site is supposedly endowed with magic, so that it is impossible to count the same number of stones twice. If you do manage to do so, then the magic is broken (or, alternatively, you are cursed by bad luck). A prophecy also states that if Long Meg were ever to be shattered, she would run with blood. It is said that when local squire Colonel Lacy attempted to destroy the stones in the 18th century, a terrifying storm broke out and the labourers fled in fear of Black Magic, refusing to return.

Having had a look around, continue along the lane through the middle of the stones. About 250m beyond the farm buildings at **Longmeg**, go through a small gate on the right to access a shady path. After a few hundred metres, the woodland on the left disappears and the Lake District's Northern Fells appear to the west – the distinctive saddleback outline of Blencathra among the peaks lining the horizon.

The path swings slightly right to hit a rough track. Go straight across – signposted Daleraven Bridge. About 800m beyond this junction, just before the path suddenly narrows considerably, take another track to the right. At

WALK 20 – LONG MEG AND HER DAUGHTERS

first, this runs between a field boundary on the left and woodland on the right. Views of the Eden Valley come and go through gaps in the hedgerow on the left. Later, you're able to look across to the North Pennines too.

Turn right when you reach the road, soon entering **Glassonby**. Follow the road round to the right through the red sandstone village, following signs for Penrith and Langwathby. Take the next surfaced lane on the right. This is a few metres short of the national speed limit sign.

The asphalt ends at the entrance to St Michael and All Angels' Church, Addingham. Go through the iron gates to enter the churchyard.

> **St Michael and All Angels** was built on its present site in the 13th century. The original church and village were washed away when the River Eden changed course in the 12th century. A Norse hogsback tombstone, two pieces of a cross shaft and some early coffin lids are kept in the church porch. They were retrieved from the site of the original church during a drought in 1913. A 10th-century, wheel-headed Anglian cross in the churchyard is also thought to have come from the earlier church.

A paved path leads round to the front of the building and out through a wall on the other side of the churchyard. Keep straight ahead through the middle of this small field. After a gate, go straight over the surfaced lane and through the large metal gate opposite. Walk along the field edge, keeping close to the wall on the right.

About 200m into the field, go through a wooden bridle-gate set back on the right. The path now runs between

WALKING IN CUMBRIA'S EDEN VALLEY

a fence on the right and an area of sparse woodland on the left. After the next gate, the path is overgrown, but it's not long before you pass through yet another gate to enter a field. Maintain a straight line, keeping to the edge of the field.

Go through a wooden gate followed quickly by a large metal gate. Now walk beside the hedgerow on the left to return to the lane that runs through the middle of **Long Meg and Her Daughters**.

Turn left to retrace your steps from the start of the walk, remembering to take the rough track straight ahead when the surfaced land bends sharp left. You then turn right at the road to walk back to **Little Salkeld**.

A 10th-century, wheel-headed cross outside St Michael and All Angels Church, Addingham

The working **corn mill** in Little Salkeld still uses water power and traditional techniques to produce a range of stone-ground organic flours. Originally built in 1745, it started life as a modest affair but then prospered when the Carlisle–Settle railway line was built. The buildings were lovingly restored by Ana and Nick Jones in 1975.

The restored corn mill in Little Salkeld

WALK 21
Melmerby Fell

Start/finish	Melmerby village (NY 615 373)
Distance	11 miles (18km)
Total ascent	707m (2320ft)
Grade	4
Time	5¾hr
Terrain	Tracks and open pathless moorland, wet in places
Maps	OS Explorer OL31 or OS Landranger 91
Transport	Bus 888 (summer only)
Facilities	Old Village Bakery; Village Stores and Tearoom; and the Shepherd's Inn, Melmerby

This route sets off from the lovely red sandstone village of Melmerby to climb its eponymous fell via quiet lanes and a lovely grassy track. You will hardly see a soul as you wander the wide, open spaces above the Eden Valley; apart from the sheep, the only company you are likely to have are the curlews, the skylarks and the occasional golden plover. The paths are few and far between on the high ground, so this walk is best saved for a clear day.

From the centre of **Melmerby** and with the Shepherd's Inn on your left, take the minor road heading south, towards Ousby and Culgaith. At the village edge, when the road bends right, turn left along a dead-end lane.

Having climbed for about 800m, the lane bends right. Leave it here by keeping straight ahead on a rough track. This winds its way between conifer plantations, home to red squirrels, and then emerges to a wonderful view of the steep western edge of the Pennine escarpment.

Eventually, go through a gate on to access land and then climb, still on the clear track, to a gate in a wall. About 110m beyond this gate, the track bends sharp left and then re-crosses the wall higher up the fell. On

WALKING IN CUMBRIA'S EDEN VALLEY

Muska Hill, left, on the descent

From the cairn and shelter at the top, you get your first view to the east, across the wide, largely uninhabited expanse of the North Pennines. This is 'big' country; full of wide, open spaces.

reaching a junction of routes near Gate Castle, which makes up part of **Melmerby Low Scar**, bear right. After this, keep right at any forks.

Go through a gate in the wall and head east-northeast towards the prominent pile of rocks straight ahead; then continue east towards the cairn on the skyline marking the top of **Knapside Hill**. As you make your way towards the summit, the mostly pathless terrain consists of a combination of grassy tufts, moss and dank green pools. You'll also pass several shake holes. ◄

Head southeast along a faint, often boggy path towards the cairn on top of Dun Edge which, at 709m (2326ft), is the highest point on **Melmerby Fell**. Swing south-southeast along the high ground, and when you reach a wall corner continue in the same direction, keeping the wall on your right. Go through the next gate in the wall to pick up a faint grassy track.

> This track marks the route of the **Maiden Way**, one of the highest Roman roads in the country. As well as being used to gain access to the lead mines of Alston Moor, this road from Bewcastle to Kirkby

130

WALK 21 – MELMERBY FELL

Thore also cut through the Brigantuem region. The Brigantes were a powerful native people who lived in this area and the Romans are thought to have used the road to exert control over them.

131

The Maiden Way

The track heads south at first, but slowly swings southwest as it gently descends. Its route is not always obvious and several boggy patches add to the difficulties. There is a cairn to guide you about 80m southwest of the next gate. About 225m beyond another gate, just after a wall corner, keep left at a waymarker post – even though the path to the right looks a lot more inviting. The bridleway, barely visible on the ground here, heads south-southwest through an area of shake holes and then veers south about 300m beyond the waymarker post. The cairned summit to your right is Muska Hill.

A few strides beyond the next gate, step up on to a raised path – the remains of an old tramway. This would've taken limestone from the **Man at Edge** quarry, located just to your left, down to the lime kiln beside Ardale Beck. Abandoning the bridleway now, follow this steeply downhill. After the next gate, follow the clear, grassy track downhill towards **Ardale Beck**. Just before the bridge, turn left along a broad, grassy path beside the large and well-preserved lime kiln.

About 300m beyond the kiln, as the slopes on your left ease back, go through the bridle-gate on the right.

Cross the bridge over **Ardale Beck** and walk east along the faint track for about 80m to reach a fingerpost. Turn right, soon heading steeply uphill on a very muddy track. At the top of the short climb, a faint track heads south-southwest across the rough pasture. Follow this. Wet and churned up by cattle, it's slow going at first.

After the next gate, descend southwest – aiming for the farm buildings at **Bank Hall**. Reaching a wall, veer right and then follow the track round to the left. On entering the farmyard, turn right and follow the concrete access track. Just before it goes over to asphalt, turn right along a rougher track – signposted Townhead. Bear left at a fork. After the next gate, although the track isn't always clear on the ground, simply keep close to the field boundary on the right as you cross a series of fields. Eventually, you're channelled on to a walled track that leads to a road at **Townhead**. Turn left along this.

You now follow a series of quiet lanes all the way back to Melmerby, 4.1km away. Turn right at a T-junction on the edge of **Ousby**. Ignoring the next turning on the right, keep to the lane with the width restriction on it. Keep right when this forks and then turn right at a T-junction to follow the road back into **Melmerby**.

The track climbs from Melmerby

WALKING IN CUMBRIA'S EDEN VALLEY

WALK 22
Kirkoswald and Raven Beck

Start/finish	Market cross in Kirkoswald (NY 554 412)
Distance	6¼ miles (10km)
Total ascent	248m (814ft)
Grade	1
Time	2¾hr
Terrain	Farmland; woodland trail; quiet country roads
Maps	OS Explorer OL5 and OL31 or OS Landrangers 86 and 91
Transport	None
Facilities	Fetherston Arms and Crown Inn, both in Kirkoswald

Setting out from the tranquil red sandstone village of Kirkoswald, this easy-going walk heads up through the pretty woodland and meadows beside Raven Beck, a tributary of the River Eden. It then crosses rolling farmland and uses quiet country lanes with great views of the surrounding hills to explore further this peaceful corner of the Eden Valley.

With your back to the market cross opposite the Fetherston Arms, turn right along the main road through **Kirkoswald** and then take the lane on the left, known as Ravenghyll – signposted High Bankhill and Park Head.

Beyond the last of the buildings, the lane narrows to a track. Then, after a kissing-gate, it narrows again as you make your way upstream on a constructed path beside **Raven Beck**. ◄ Beyond a second kissing-gate, bear right at a fork. Almost immediately, you'll see a trail going off to the right. Ignore this. The woods here are truly gorgeous in spring when the ground is covered in a carpet of white ramsons, giving off their pungent, garlic-like aroma.

All too soon though, the trees are left behind as you cross a stile. There's no path on the ground now; keep close to the fence on your right as you cross three fields.

In spring, the slope on the left – Millie Bank – is a riot of colour, full of wildflowers and butterflies.

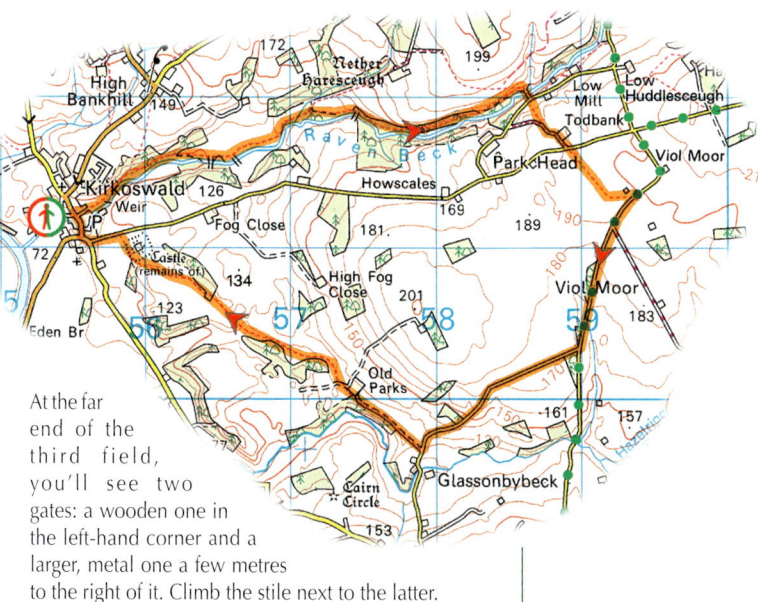

At the far end of the third field, you'll see two gates: a wooden one in the left-hand corner and a larger, metal one a few metres to the right of it. Climb the stile next to the latter.

Keeping reasonably close to the trees on your right as you cross a flat, grassy area, you eventually reach a kissing-gate next to the beck. Once through this, you're back in woodland again, following a narrow trail upstream.

On the path beside Raven Beck

135

WALKING IN CUMBRIA'S EDEN VALLEY

Reaching a wider track, bear left. Just before a metal bridge, turn left again, picking up another narrow trail.

About 300m after leaving the woods via a stile in a wall, you finally cross Raven Beck via a wooden, railed footbridge. Go up the embankment and turn right along the lane. Almost immediately, take the overgrown path rising to the left. Once over the stile, keep straight ahead. You'll soon see a damp ditch with a fence and wall to the left of it. The ditch itself is impassable; keep to the right of it and follow it steadily uphill.

Reaching a fence, carefully cross the low, single line of barbed wire on your left to access a stile in the now considerably drier ditch. Cross this and continue uphill with a wall on your left and a fence on the right. ◄

The views now include the North Pennines to the left and, glimpsed briefly, the distinctive 'saddleback' outline of Blencathra some way to the southwest.

The path is very overgrown as it swings left, but the difficulties are soon over as it emerges on a farm lane. Bear right along this to reach a narrow road. Go straight across, through a large metal gate and walk with the wall on your right. After two more large gates, turn sharp left along the field edge. A wooden stile gives access to an overgrown trail around the edge of a tiny patch of woodland.

Sheep grazing near Viol Moor

WALK 22 – KIRKOSWALD AND RAVEN BECK

Turn right along the road – over **Viol Moor**. Take the next road on the right. With views ahead to the Lake District fells, you soon begin losing height. At the bottom of the long, slow descent, turn right along **Old Parks**' surfaced track – signposted Kirkoswald. Turn left after entering the farmyard and then leave it via the left-hand of the two gates ahead.

> The bird-bath on a hillock up to the left is a memorial to the **Rev George Bramwell Evens**, a Minister of the Methodist Church better known as 'Romany of the BBC'. He presented *Out with Romany* on BBC Radio's *Children's Hour* in the 1930s and 1940s, and is generally regarded as Britain's first natural history broadcaster. He spent a lot of time at Old Parks Farm watching and studying the wildlife, and his ashes were scattered here after he died in 1943.

After the next gate, leave the track and instead walk beside the fence on the right. Go through a gate and then continue with a fenced area of woodland on your left. About 230m beyond the gate, bear slightly right – away from the trees and towards a gate to the right of another patch of woodland. Once over the stile beside this gate, cross a second stile to enter the trees. A faint trail, difficult to make out at times, heads through the trees, never straying far from the fence to the right. After crossing another stile, walk with the fence on your left and then cross a stile beside a gate.

Pass to the right of the fenced hillock straight ahead. When the fence on the left bends sharp left, keep straight on – along a faint path. This disappears before reaching a water trough. Go through a metal farm gate a few metres to the right of the trough. Pass to the right of a pond and through another gate to access a grassy path between two fences. This ends at a gate. Once through this, turn left to walk beside the fence on the left. Follow the fence round to the right and then cross a stile to access a grassy track.

You can now see the remains of **Kirkoswald Castle**, partially obscured by trees, on your right. To the left,

Life returns to the woods beside Raven Beck at the start of spring

sitting on top of a small hill, is the unusual detached bell tower of St Oswald's Church.

Turn left along the road and then right at two subsequent junctions. Follow the road back over **Raven Beck** to return to the market cross in **Kirkoswald**.

KIRKOSWALD

Once a thriving market town, Kirkoswald gets its name from the church of St Oswald. Oswald was the King of Northumbria, who travelled around the north of England with St Aidan in the seventh century, trying to convert the inhabitants to Christianity. Local legend has it that St Aidan saw people worshipping at a well here and decided to build a Christian church on top of it. The early church would have been a wooden one, but the current structure dates from 1897. The well is under the nave, but there is access to it on the external west wall, where a metal cup sits attached to a chain. The churchyard also contains some interesting Saxon grave covers.

An unusual feature of St Oswald's is its bell tower, which is actually perched on top of a hill about 140m from the church itself.

Opposite the entrance to the church is the College, a beautiful house originally built as a pele tower in 1450. It was converted into a college for priests by Thomas de Dacre in the 1520s, but was closed in the 1540s following the Dissolution of the Monasteries. It then became the home of the Fetherstonhaugh family, who had previously lived at the castle.

WALK 23
Armathwaite and Coombs Wood

Start/finish	Duke's Head Hotel, Armathwaite (NY 505 460)
Distance	3½ miles (5.5km)
Total ascent	186m (610ft)
Grade	1
Time	1½hr
Terrain	Good tracks and quiet country roads
Maps	OS Explorer OL5 or OS Landranger 86
Transport	Armathwaite is on the Settle–Carlisle railway
Facilities	Duke's Head Hotel and Fox and Pheasant Inn, Armathwaite

This short-but-sweet walk starts with a peaceful stroll through Coombs Wood. With the sparkling Eden far below, it heads ever deeper into the forest. But the delights don't end there; after a short section of road walking, it reaches one of Cumbria's more off-the-beaten-track hamlets – Longdales – and then heads north along a seemingly forgotten track between hedgerows that are a riot of colour in the autumn. It makes for a perfect Sunday morning stroll, and if you time things carefully, you should arrive back in Armathwaite just in time for pub opening.

Starting with your back to the Duke's Head Hotel in **Armathwaite**, turn right along the road. Immediately after the road bridge over the **River Eden**, cross the stile on the left and follow the path round to the left and under the bridge so that you are heading upstream with the river on your right along a clear, tree-lined path. ▶

Having followed the riverside path for 650m, you draw level with the renovated buildings of Mill Farm on the other side of some rapids. Bear left at the faint fork here, heading uphill. Then, in a further 100m, you will see a wall heading up the slope on your left. Turn sharp left here to climb beside it. Before long, you step up on to

Look for Armathwaite Castle on the opposite bank. This pele tower was converted into a country house in 1752 by William Sanderson.

WALKING IN CUMBRIA'S EDEN VALLEY

The tree-lined path beside the River Eden on the edge of Armathwaite

a clearer path. (There is a stile on the left here.) Turn right to follow the wide path into the forest. (You soon pass one of the Eden Benchmark sculptures, 'Vista' by Graeme Mitcheson, carved from St Bees sandstone.)

Ignore any track turnings on the right; simply keep ascending steadily through **Coombs Wood**, surrounded by tall, slender conifers swaying in the wind. Occasionally, there are snatched glimpses of the River Eden far below – flowing through a beautiful valley, the graceful, curvaceous sides of which are covered in woodland and verdant fields and meadows. Beyond the metal gate, turn left along the road and then take the next lane on the right. Immediately after passing the cottages in **Longdales**, turn left along a track. This climbs to a high point of about 170m, from where you get a superb

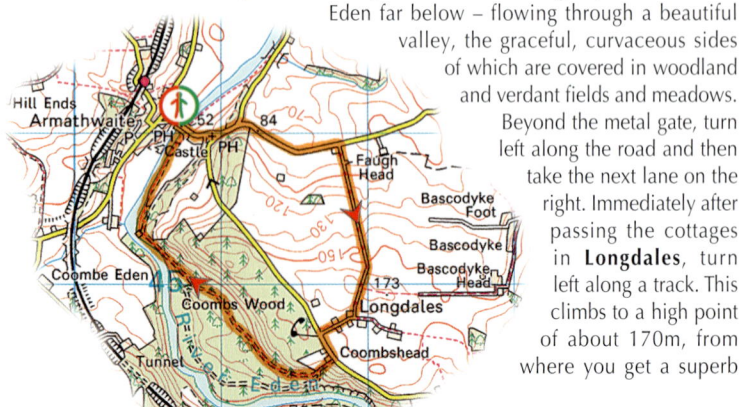

WALK 23 – ARMATHWAITE AND COOMBS WOOD

view of the rolling farmland to the north and the Pennines to the east. Those views stay with you as you continue straight ahead between hedgerows.

Turn left along the road. Follow it back across the River Eden and retrace your steps into **Armathwaite**.

Rolling farmland at the foot of the Pennines

WALKING IN CUMBRIA'S EDEN VALLEY

WALK 24
Croglin and Newbiggin

Start/finish	Croglin (NY 573 471)
Distance	5 miles (8.2km)
Total ascent	220m (720ft)
Grade	2
Time	2¾hr
Terrain	Tracks; farmland; quiet country roads
Maps	OS Explorer OL5 or OS Landranger 86
Transport	None
Facilities	Blue Bell Inn, Newbiggin

In Cumbria the words 'Croglin' and 'vampire' go together like 'Bram' and 'Stoker'. And wandering the tracks and paths linking this tiny fellside settlement with nearby Newbiggin in the depths of winter, it is not hard to see how the story of the Croglin vampire has lingered so long in this bleak but somehow beautiful area tucked in at the very foot of the Pennine escarpment. However, come the spring, the undead couldn't be further from your thoughts as you wander the high track between the two hamlets, listening to the skylarks celebrating the change of season and the ewes calling to their lambs.

Head southwest along the signposted track that starts at the former Robin Hood pub in **Croglin**. With fairly solid ground underfoot, the walking is easy, allowing you plenty of time to enjoy the views across the Eden Valley to the Lake District fells.

The track, which goes over to grass in its later stages, eventually ends at a metal gate. Go through and head in roughly the same direction – towards a wooden step stile in the fence opposite. A faint path then continues through the grass, soon crossing a small beck and climbing the short embankment to reach a wall. Walk with the wall on your left until you reach a gate providing access to a quiet road.

WALK 24 – CROGLIN AND NEWBIGGIN

Turn right and walk along the asphalt for nearly 2km, passing a turning on the right for Croglin at **Hazelgill**, and then a turning on the left. Soon after the latter you will see **Cairnhead Farm** on your right. About 140m beyond these buildings, go through a waymarked gap in the wall up to your right.

Walk with the wall on your left. At the top of the field, cross a stile and a farm track to reach a gate. Go through this and continue with the wall on your left. At the bottom of the slope, cross two stiles in quick succession followed by a plank bridge. Now head up the slope with a wall and fence on your right. Turn left at the road. Just after passing the

The Northern Fells are visible in the distance

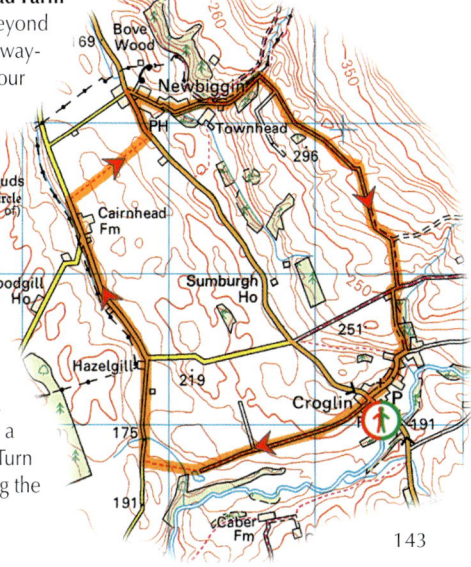

WALKING IN CUMBRIA'S EDEN VALLEY

Blue Bell Inn in **Newbiggin**, turn right along a lane leading further into the hamlet. Follow this almost to its end.

> There are dozens of places called **Newbiggin** all over the north of England, including at least five in the area covered by this guidebook. It simply means 'new building' and originates from Old Norse.

As you approach **Townhead** you will see a track heading up to the left on to access land. Ignore this; continue for just a few more metres to pick up a signposted bridleway climbing to the left.

The clear, wide track climbs at a moderate angle through the wooded ravine with Newbiggin Beck over to the left. As the track emerges from the trees follow it round to the right, ignoring the footpath through the gate straight ahead. The views become more and more interesting as you gradually gain height. The Northern Fells can be clearly seen to the right, with Blencathra's saddleback outline especially obvious from this angle. Behind you, the Scottish hills look impressive, with Criffel dominating the scene. As you reach the top of the first rise, the

The high track between Newbiggin and Croglin

WALK 24 – CROGLIN AND NEWBIGGIN

panorama manages simultaneously to be both beautiful and bleak. ▶

Eventually, soon after passing through the first gate reached on the track, bear right as another track comes down from the left. Beyond a second gate, the track drops to a junction. Turn right here and then go left – passing the buildings at Plantation Nook on your right. Reaching an asphalt lane, bear right and follow it back into **Croglin**.

Looking to the right over the verdant Eden Valley, a long line of misty Lake District fells fills the horizon, but straight ahead and to the left are the peat moorlands of the Pennines.

THE CROGLIN VAMPIRE

No visit to Croglin would be complete without a retelling of the blood-curdling tale of the Croglin vampire. Depending on which version of the story you hear, the terrifying events happened in either the 19th century or just after the English Civil War, and the scene of the vampire attack was either Croglin Low Hall or Croglin Grange.

The owners of the house, the Fishers, had let it to two brothers and a sister, the Cranswells. One balmy summer night, the sister was savagely attacked by a mysterious creature that somehow managed to get into her bedroom and bite her throat. Several months later the creature returned, but this time Miss Cranswell's terrified screams alerted her brothers and they came rushing to her aid with their pistols drawn. One of the brothers shot the creature in the leg and it fled, scrambled over the churchyard wall and disappeared into a vault.

The next day the brothers and several brave villagers went into the vault and discovered that all but one of the coffins had been smashed to pieces. The one that remained intact turned out to contain shrivelled remains with the marks of a recent pistol shot in one leg. They set fire to the coffin and its contents, and the creature was never seen again.

Walking in Cumbria's Eden Valley

WALK 25
Wetheral

Start/finish	Wetheral Parish Church (NY 468 543)
Distance	4½ miles (7km)
Total ascent	131m (430ft)
Grade	1
Time	2hr
Terrain	Riverside paths; woodland trails; farmland; quiet lanes
Maps	OS Explorer 315 or OS Landranger 86
Transport	Wetheral is served by bus 74/75 and the Carlisle to Newcastle railway
Facilities	Crown Hotel, The Wheatsheaf, Fantails and The Posting Pot coffee lounge, all in Wetheral

This walk heads to the village of Wetheral to spend a couple of hours in the attractive countryside to the east of Carlisle. Having explored a few historic sights on the edge of the village, including some mysterious caves cut into the red sandstone cliffs high above the River Eden, and enjoyed a stroll in the National Trust woods, the route heads away from Wetheral. It now winds its way through the farmland to the north of the village, delighting in views of the North Pennines and one snatched glimpse of the Lake District's Northern Fells.

With your back to the lych gate of Holy Trinity Church, turn right along the road and then immediately left – signposted to **Wetheral Priory Gatehouse**. You'll see Corby Castle on the other side of the **River Eden** and then reach the old gatehouse. With the stairwell on the northeastern side of the building open to the public, it's well worth a visit.

WETHERAL PRIORY

Set up by a small community of Benedictine monks in 1106 and dedicated to the Holy Trinity and St Constantine, this priory was one of the earliest monastic foundations in this area after the Norman Conquest, it was established when

WALK 25 – WETHERAL

Ranulf Meschin, the first Norman lord of Cumberland, granted the manor to the abbot of St Mary's in York.

Although it was only a small priory, with no more than a dozen monks at any one time, it was obviously important locally. It even played host to the Prince of Wales, the future King Edward II, in 1301 and again in 1307 when his father, Edward I, moved the seals of the crown to nearby Lanercost (Walk 28).

Criminals could seek sanctuary within a special area in Wetheral, delineated by a series of small stone crosses. The only catch was that they had to ring the bells of the parish church and vow to keep the peace – a small price to pay for immunity from arrest. In 1342, Edward III offered a pardon to all those claiming sanctuary in Wetheral if they would join him and his armies in the fight against the Scots.

Much of the priory fell into ruin after Henry VIII's Dissolution of the Monasteries, although the red sandstone gatehouse, dating from the 15th century, continued to be used as a fortified vicarage during the 16th and 17thcenturies. This is all that remains of the priory today. Visitors can enter the building free of charge most days except for during the Christmas and New Year period. For more information, visit www.english-heritage.org.uk.

Wetheral Woods

WALKING IN CUMBRIA'S EDEN VALLEY

From the gatehouse, continue along the minor road for another 140m and then go through the metal kissing-gate on the left. Walk downhill beside a fence, soon entering the National Trust's Wetheral Woods on a clear, but occasionally muddy path. You'll see a couple of paths heading down to the left, but you should stay on the higher path until it splits. When it does so, bear left. You'll return to this fork after visiting **St Constantine's Cells**. The path leads, in a short while, down some steps and into the caves hewn from the red sandstone above the **River Eden**.

The steps leading from St Constantine's Cells

St Constantine's Cells were probably used as storage chambers by the Benedictine monks from the nearby priory, possibly as a place to hide their valuables during cross-border raids. More colourful theories claim the caves were used as a hermitage, but there is no clear evidence to suggest anyone ever lived in them.

Having explored the site, return to the point at which the path split and then, almost immediately, bear right at the next fork – heading downhill. Before long, you leave National Trust land via a kissing-gate and continue on a path beside the **River Eden**. Drop to the sandy riverbank opposite the ornate gardens of **Corby Castle** and you'll see Wetheral Viaduct ahead.

> **Corby Castle** probably started life as a wooden building in the 11th century, and then a stone pele tower was constructed in the 13th century. What you see today, including the classical façade, is mostly 19th century.

Continue beside the river to a stone-carved bench, another of the Eden Benchmark sculptures. This one is called Flight of Fancy and was created by Tim Shutter. Turn left soon after the bench and then take the lane on the right. As soon as you pass beneath the viaduct, take the path on the right. Another short stretch of riverside walking ensues before the trail returns to the quiet lane. Turn right to continue in the same direction as before.

For a five-minute detour to St Cuthbert's Well, take the signposted trail on the left a few metres after re-joining the asphalt and then turn left along a broad track. The steps down to the holy well are on the left in about 65m. ▶

The age of the restored well is unknown, although it's said to pre-date the founding of the 12th-century priory. St Cuthbert, most closely associated with Lindisfarne in Northumberland, is thought to have visited nearby Carlisle on at least two occasions.

Back on the main route – continuing north along the quiet lane – you'll quickly reach a junction with the **B6263**. Turn right here. Having walked along the asphalt for about 800m, turn left through a farm gate to access a rough track between hedgerows. Keep straight on as a path goes off to 'Warwick' to the right. When the track ends, go through the large metal gate and bear right to walk beside the fence. Ignore a permissive path going through a gate on the right almost straight away. At a second waymarked set of gates, bear left. There's no path on the ground here – or fence to guide you – but you should head roughly south-southwest, up and over the hillock to reach a metal kissing-gate in the far corner of the field. Once through this, walk along the field edge with a fence on your left. ◄

> This is the highest point on the walk and provides a good view of the North Pennines to the east.

After the next small gate, a faint trail follows the top edge of the ground sloping away to the left, heading in the direction of a detached house on the edge of **Wetheral**. Go through the kissing-gate beside the house, turn right and then go right again at the road.

Walk along the asphalt for 370m and then leave the road by going left through a kissing-gate on a sharp bend to the right – signposted Wetheral and Scotby Road. Follow the fenced, shady path round to the left and then out to a stile. Resisting the lure of the lovely grassy track to the right, cross the stile. Crossing a couple more stiles along the way, walk beside the field boundary on your left until you reach the railway. Skiddaw and the Northern Fells can just be seen above the treetops far to the southwest.

Carefully cross the railway line and turn left along the rough track. Passing some farm buildings along the way, this track leads all the way back into Wetheral. It comes out close to a junction with the **B6263**. Turn right along this main road through the village. Immediately after passing a turning on the left for the railway station, take the next road on the left. You'll have the village green on your right now. Follow the road down to the left to return to the parish church where the walk started.

WALK 26
Talkin Fell and Simmerson Hill

Start/finish	Blacksmiths Arms, Talkin (NY 549 573). Please park considerately nearby in the village
Distance	6¼ miles (10km)
Total ascent	390m (1280ft)
Grade	2–3
Time	3¾hr
Terrain	Good tracks; quiet lanes; open moorland, wet in places
Maps	OS Explorer 315 or OS Landranger 86
Transport	None
Facilities	Blacksmiths Arms, Talkin

They say good things come in small packages and that seems particularly apt for this walk onto two very low-lying tops in the Pennines. After a fairly gentle climb from Talkin village, you reach one of the best viewpoints in this part of Cumbria. Topped by a collection of tall cairns and a trig pillar, Talkin Fell (1250ft) is a wonderful place to stand at the end of a sunny spring afternoon, admiring the views and listening to the curlews returning to their nesting sites. The route then crosses to nearby Simmerson Hill (1312ft) before dropping into Geltsdale, one of the loveliest and loneliest of North Pennine valleys.

Stand facing the Blacksmiths Arms in **Talkin** village and take the quiet road to the left of the pub, towards Forest Head. After about 500m take the road turning on your right. The road swings sharp left and then comes to an abrupt end just after the buildings at **Talkin Head**. ▸

Continue straight ahead on the rough track, climbing steadily. You'll pass a signposted bridleway to the right of the track. Ignore it at this stage, but this will form part of your return route later in the day. Surprisingly quickly, your surroundings take on a much wilder nature as you look up into Geltsdale. You'll also catch your first glimpse of the tall cairns on top of Talkin Fell.

Talkin comes from the Celtic word talcan meaning 'brow of the hill'.

GELTSDALE

Geltsdale is part of a 5400-hectare nature reserve run by the RSPB. It is one of the few sites in England where the rare hen harrier can still be found. Other breeding birds include merlin, golden plover, ring ouzel, curlew, lapwing, redshank and snipe. More than 300 species of flowering plants have been recorded, including national rarities such as pale forget-me-not and spring sandwort.

There is even a chance of seeing the beautiful, but increasingly rare, black grouse – if you're extremely lucky. These birds have suffered a devastating decline in numbers in England over the last hundred years or so, mostly due to over-grazing and loss of habitat. They are now confined to the North Pennines and other parts of Northumberland and North Yorkshire.

Visit soon after daybreak in spring and you might catch sight of the male birds 'lekking'. The 'lek' is the birds' famous flamboyant display, which the females attend to choose a mate. In this impressive dance the males spread their tail feathers, showing off their magnificent, glossy black plumage, extend their wings and inflate the distinctive red 'combs' above each eye. They crouch and circle the ground and spar with each other in a bid to dominate the site and become the females' choice of mate.

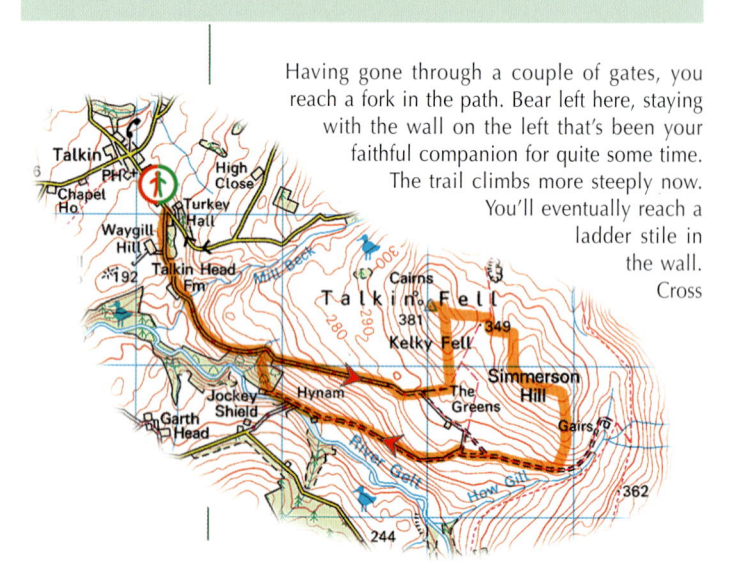

Having gone through a couple of gates, you reach a fork in the path. Bear left here, staying with the wall on the left that's been your faithful companion for quite some time. The trail climbs more steeply now. You'll eventually reach a ladder stile in the wall. Cross

WALK 26 – TALKIN FELL AND SIMMERSON HILL

The summit of Talkin Fell

this and you will see the trig pillar of **Talkin Fell** straight ahead. ▶

From the summit, retrace your steps across the ladder stile. Follow the path you took earlier, but only for a few metres; as soon as it forks, bear left, now heading away from the wall. The narrow path gently descends and crosses a flat, boggy area, staying parallel with a fence on the right.

At the base of the short slope on to **Simmerson Hill**, go through the gate on the right. (This is the second gate in the fence.) Almost immediately, turn left (east). There is a faint trail here, parallel with the fence on the left, but it's hard to spot.

Climb the small jumble of rocks forming a rim around the entire western edge of **Simmerson Hill**. Turn right along a path following the edge of this heathery fell, enjoying great views of Geltsdale as you make your way south and then southeast. On reaching a fence, bear right to head downhill. The path is less obvious now, but it follows the line of the fence down to a much wider, clearer track, along which you turn right.

Just beyond the summit trig pillar the decidedly eerie tall cairns stand guard along the western edge of the fell.

On Simmerson Hill

The old mine workers' cottages at **Gairs** may just be discernible in the valley below as you descend from Simmerson Hill. The Gairs mine formed part of the East Cumberland Coalfield, which is thought to be one of the oldest in England, possibly even worked by the Romans. At its peak in the 1920s, almost 200 men worked at Gairs, producing around 70,000 tonnes of coal per year. It was abandoned in 1936. The mine's rail line, which forms part of one of the earliest industrial railways in the world, ran to nearby Hallbankgate.

After about 500m keep left at a fork in the track. Far below, the noisy River Gelt rushes through the wooded valley. You soon join a path coming down from the right and, before you know it, the track drops to the edge of the **River Gelt** near some buildings. Continue along the clear track on the northern side of the river. The gorge here is particularly spectacular, as a huge volume of water tries to make its way through the narrowest of gaps.

When you reach the gate leading on to private land at **Low Hynam**, bear right to head along a gated track that climbs steadily through the woods to emerge on to the track that you followed earlier in the walk. Turn left along it and retrace your steps to **Talkin**.

WALK 27
Talkin Tarn and the Gelt

Start/finish	Talkin Tarn car park (NY 543 590)
Distance	7¾ miles (12.5km)
Total ascent	348m (1142ft)
Grade	2
Time	4½hr
Terrain	Farm paths; woodland; tracks; quiet lanes
Maps	OS Explorer 315 or OS Landranger 86
Transport	The route passes close to Brampton railway station, which is on the Carlisle–Newcastle line
Facilities	Blacksmiths Arms, Talkin; Boathouse Tea Room at Talkin Tarn; public toilets at Talkin Tarn

'If local people eat there, it's likely to be a good restaurant', so tourists are told wherever they travel. And, if Talkin Tarn and Gelt Woods are anything to go by, the same is true for beauty spots. 'If local people walk there...' On warm summer Sundays the car park at Talkin Tarn gets very busy as the population of the surrounding towns and villages descends on this attractive body of water, while the paths through Gelt Woods are full of dog-walkers and families out for a stroll.

The best times to visit are the beginning and end of the day when the light on the tarn is simply magical, and photographers line up with their tripods to capture the mood. Autumn colours seem particularly vibrant in the fascinating gorge cut by the often tumultuous River Gelt, and this is also a good time of year to spot red squirrels stocking up on food for the winter.

From the main pay-and-display car park, head down to **Talkin Tarn** and turn left to begin walking along the path beside the water. You soon pass the boathouse, which is home to a tearoom and one of the oldest non-collegiate rowing clubs in the country.

Talkin Tarn, fed by underground streams, is glacial in origin. It is a kettle-hole lake, formed when a block of ice broke away from the main glacier and

Beside Talkin Tarn

was left stranded in the sandy deposits left by the meltwater. When the ice-block eventually melted, it left a depression filled with water.

Talkin Tarn Amateur Rowing Club celebrated its 150th birthday in 2009, making it the second oldest rowing club in the north of England after the Tyne Rowing Club. Races were first held on the tarn in the 1850s. Over the years the club's members have competed in the Olympic Games, international regattas, the World Rowing Championships and World Masters Rowing Championships in various countries.

Beyond the trees, the tarn-side path swings right. Leave it here by turning left, towards a kissing-gate in the field corner. Beyond this, the fenced path negotiates a wet area via stone slabs before continuing between the meadows to another gate. Beyond this, the path swings right to skirt some woodland. After one more gate, it works its way round the bottom edge of a field before climbing to a gate on the edge of **Farlam**. Once through this, turn sharp right along the road – towards Talkin and Castle Carrock.

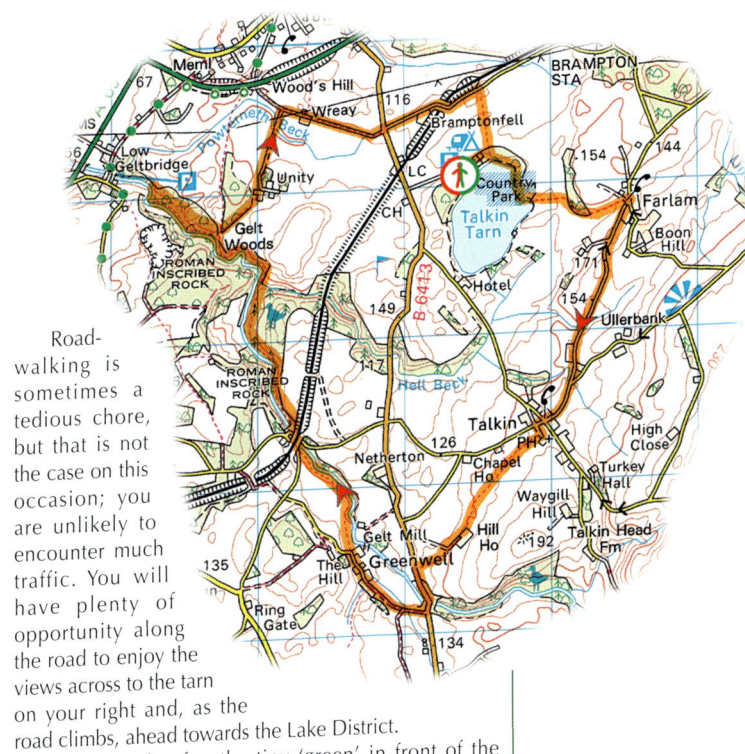

Road-walking is sometimes a tedious chore, but that is not the case on this occasion; you are unlikely to encounter much traffic. You will have plenty of opportunity along the road to enjoy the views across to the tarn on your right and, as the road climbs, ahead towards the Lake District.

Immediately after the tiny 'green' in front of the Blacksmiths Arms in **Talkin**, turn left along a gravel track. As you enter the parking area at the side of the pub, you will see a well-hidden set of steps in the wall corner on your right. This marks the start of the next section of footpath. Once over the wall, follow the narrow trail through the trees, cross a private driveway and then climb the stile in the fence. Now make for the small gate on the other side of this paddock and then continue in the same direction through the next field. Go through the metal gate and walk with the fence on your right until you join a clear track.

This takes you up towards the farm buildings at **Hill House**. Follow the waymarkers through the yard, in front of the ornate Victorian farmhouse and then on to a lane. When the lane swings sharp right, bear left on to a grassy

The pub at Talkin bathed in late evening sunshine

track between a hedge and a wall. At the end of this, go through the gate immediately in front of you, bear half-right and drop to a stile beside a gate.

Turn left along the road and follow it as it drops to a bridge over the **River Gelt**. You then climb slightly and, 100m beyond the bridge, turn right along a wide track – signposted Greenwell. After crossing a stream, bear right to pass through a pair of green metal gates. Bear right at the house at Greenwell Meadows. The path descends to a gravel area in front of a row of delightfully isolated cottages at **Greenwell**. Now keep straight ahead, through another gate and on to a surfaced lane.

GREENWELL

This hamlet is home to Gelt Mill, which was built in 1776. Until the end of the 19th century it took water from the Gelt via a series of sluice gates, but the works were destroyed by a flood in 1894. It was then driven by water from Castle Carrock Beck. The mill was closed in 1939 and then converted into a private home in the 1980s. The mill pond, sluice gates, shafts and cog wheels have all been restored.

A skeleton in full battle gear was once found in a tree near this pretty hamlet. It is thought he had been fleeing from the bloody battle between followers of Mary Queen of Scots and royal cavalrymen in 1570. The three-day clash, sometimes known as the Battle of Gelt Bridge, resulted in the slaughter of many hundreds of men, with the rebel forces being beaten. This was just one of many skirmishes involving northern Catholic noblemen seeking to depose Queen Elizabeth I and replace her with her cousin Mary during the so-called Rising of the North.

The main rebellion in 1569 was led by the earls of Westmorland and Northumberland, who occupied Durham and Barnard Castle but had to abandon their plans to lay siege to York. The battle at Gelt Bridge involved Leonard Dacre of Naworth Castle who had tried to be seen as remaining loyal to Elizabeth during the rising. However, she wasn't fooled and sent her cousin Lord Hunsdon to capture Dacre. Hunsdon was outnumbered almost two to one by Dacre's men, and failed to take Naworth Castle. As the royal army retreated to Carlisle, Dacre attacked them and it was at Gelt Bridge that his men were defeated. Dacre fled, via Scotland, to Flanders where he ended his days on a pension from Philip II of Spain.

Walk along the asphalt until the lane bends left just after the final building on your right. Leave it here by crossing the stile beside the gate on your right. You now follow a peaceful stretch of river for just over 800m, crossing several fields. The path isn't always clear on the ground; simply follow the **River Gelt** downstream, eventually passing to the right of a fenced gas compound.

When you reach the road near the impressive **Gelt Bridge Viaduct**, completed in 1835, turn right to pass under the arch and then right again at the junction. Immediately after crossing the road bridge over the river, turn left through the gate into **Gelt Woods**. You now walk through the beautiful, wooded gorge with the rushing River Gelt on your left and tall red sandstone cliffs on either side. ▸

There are several trails off into the woods on your right, but you should ignore all of them. Having walked the main woodland path for about 1.7km, you'll reach a clearly waymarked fork where you should again keep

The woodland, with alder and ash on the lower slopes and birch and oak higher up, is home to red squirrels, roe deer and a variety of birdlife including kingfishers, woodpeckers, chiffchaffs and dippers.

left. After the fork, you cross a 'causeway' at the base of low cliffs.

> High above the causeway is the Roman **Written Rock of Gelt**. Dating back to AD207, it records the quarry workings of Roman soldiers belonging to the Second Legion. Tennyson wrote of the rock: 'The Vexillary hath left crag-carven o'er the streaming Gelt' in his *Idylls of the King*. Sadly, the steps that once led to the rock high above the main path have been badly eroded and the route up to it is dangerous.

Beyond the 'causeway', the river forces itself through an unusual winding channel through the smooth bedrock and then makes a sharp bend to the right. (The curious potholes in the opposite bank of the river at the bend have been formed over thousands of years as stones, spinning in the fast-moving water, have eroded the sandstone bedrock.) Soon after the river's sharp bend to the right, the path climbs to a carved wooden bench. Leave the Gelt by turning sharp right, almost back on yourself on a wide path running parallel with the path you were just following, but at a higher point in the woods. (Ignore the trail climbing beside the fence.)

At a junction of paths near a fence, turn left. Almost immediately, bear right – through a metal kissing-gate. Follow the wall on your right to a farm building at **Unity**. Keep to the left of the building to reach a lane. Turn left, ignoring the track up to the farmhouse in a short while. At a T-junction, turn right. Beyond the old farm at **Wreay**, this track goes through a gate and continues between hedgerows. Go straight over the road and continue along the surfaced lane opposite. Soon after crossing the railway bridge, the road rises and then dips. As it starts to head downhill, go through the gate on the right. Follow the vehicle track, but when this disintegrates into nothing more than muddy ruts, keep to the fence on your right. After a kissing-gate leading into **Talkin Tarn Country Park**, turn right. As the track passes a toilet block, swing right to re-enter the car park where the walk started.

WALK 28
Quarry Beck and Ridgewood

Start/finish	Parking and picnic area on the north side of Lanercost Bridge over the River Irthing (NY 553 633). If approaching from the south, watch for a gap in the hedges on your left just over the bridge, giving access to the parking area.
Distance	4 miles (6.5km)
Total ascent	114m (375ft)
Grade	1–2
Time	2hr
Terrain	Woodland paths; tracks; country roads
Maps	OS Explorer 315 or OS Landranger 86
Transport	Brampton is served by bus 685
Facilities	Lanercost Tearooms

Beautiful Quarry Beck is hidden away in a peaceful, wooded valley just to the south of Lanercost, while Ridgewood is a line of high ground with surprisingly good views over the surrounding countryside. Linking the two via quiet country roads, this walk forms a gentle stroll. Bluebells add to the pleasure in May.

Starting from the parking and picnic area beside the pretty **River Irthing**, cross the old **Lanercost Bridge**. ▶ On reaching Abbey Bridge House, continue in the same direction along the road. About 130m beyond Abbey Bridge House, walk between the wooden barriers on the left to access a path through the woods.

Dropping into the peaceful, secluded gorge, you pass waterfalls, small meadows and occasional outcrops of gorgeous red sandstone as you follow **Quarry Beck** upstream. Always keep to the lowest path, ignoring any trails heading up to the right. The peace is temporarily broken as you cross the road leading into the stoneworks,

> The old bridge was built in 1724 to replace earlier bridges that were destroyed by floods. Traffic stopped using it in 1962 when the less attractive road bridge was built next to it.

Walking in Cumbria's Eden Valley

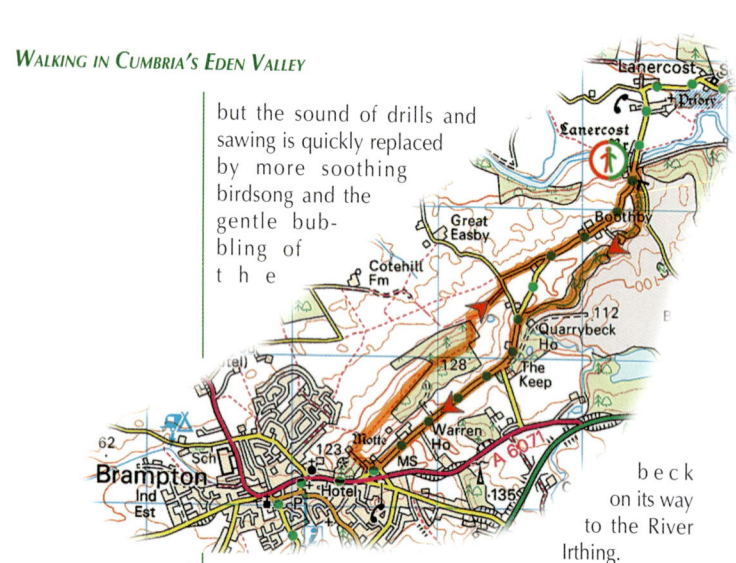

but the sound of drills and sawing is quickly replaced by more soothing birdsong and the gentle bubbling of the beck on its way to the River Irthing.

You sadly part company with the beck as you draw level with some homes on the other side of the water. The path now heads up through the trees to reach the road, along which you turn left. There is a grass verge to the left of the road at

The view from The Ridgewood

WALK 28 – QUARRY BECK AND RIDGEWOOD

first, after which you'll pick up a footpath on the other side. This leads all the way into **Brampton**.

Just 120m after passing a road turning to the left at the edge of the green on the outskirts of the town, turn right up a broad but rough track – signposted 'Ridge Walk'. At the top of the rise, bear right to pass in front of Moat Cottage. Go through an old metal kissing-gate and then follow a line of beautiful beech trees along the crest of the low ridge. ▶

Walk with the fence on your right at first, but then go through a pedestrian gate in it to continue with it on your left. The route now passes through a lovely area of woodland, known as The Ridgewood, which is particularly gorgeous in the autumn. Keep straight ahead, until you reach a fence corner near the woodland edge. Continue with the fence on your right for a further 30m and then bear left, down a narrow path that weaves its way through the trees. At the bottom of this path, bear right – through the metal kissing-gate. Go through another gate in a few metres and you'll eventually find yourself at the roadside.

Turn left and then right. You then bear left to re-join the main road. It's now an easy stroll back to **Lanercost Bridge**, but be careful because the road has several bends on it.

> You are less than 150m above sea level here and yet the views are wonderful. You have the Pennines over to the right, but it's the panorama to the left that really catches the eye, backed by the Scottish hills.

LANERCOST PRIORY

For an interesting detour, continue just 500m along the road to visit atmospheric Lanercost Priory. This was founded by Augustinian canons in 1166. Being so close to the Scottish border, it has had a turbulent history. The priory suffered its first raid in 1280 following a visit by Edward I, but the most damaging attack came in 1346 when King David II of Scotland ransacked the monastic buildings, desecrated the priory church and wasted lands belonging to the priory.

Lanercost's unusual claim to fame is that for five months in 1306–7, a dying Edward I ruled his kingdom from here, having summoned Parliament to Carlisle and moved the seals of the crown to Lanercost, effectively making it England's capital.

Lanercost Priory

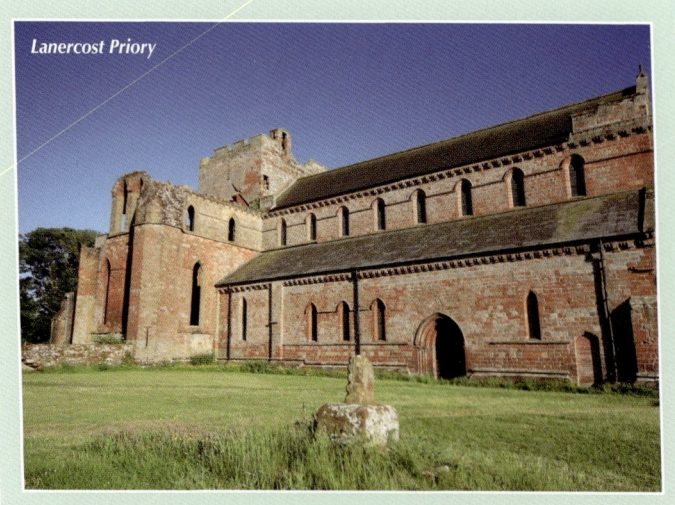

During the Dissolution of the Monasteries in 1536, the site was granted to Sir Thomas Dacre who converted the west range buildings into a private residence. In the middle of the 19th century, the ruins of the nave were restored and turned into an attractive parish church by the renowned architect Anthony Salvin. The substantial remains of the north and south transepts, the choir, the sanctuary and the cellarium are now in the care of English Heritage, and are open daily to the public from April to October, and winter weekends. There is an admission fee.

WALK 29
Burgh Marsh

Start/finish	St Michael's Church, Burgh by Sands (NY 328 591)
Distance	7 miles (11.5km)
Total ascent	99m (325ft)
Grade	1–2
Time	3hr
Terrain	Quiet lanes; open grazing; muddy riverbank, overgrown in places; farmland
Maps	OS Explorer 315 or OS Landranger 85
Transport	Bus 93/93A
Facilities	Greyhound Inn, Burgh by Sands

With the now brackish waters of the River Eden lapping up against the edge of immense salt-marshes, this route gives walkers a sense of the Solway's wide open spaces as well as a glimpse of the Scottish hills in the distance. This is part of the Solway Coast Area of Outstanding Natural Beauty, designated in 1964 and stretching from Rockcliffe in the northeast to Maryport in the west.

As long as you check the tide tables and weather conditions before setting out and don't stray too far from established routes, the Solway salt-marshes can be a fascinating and beautiful area to explore. Steeped in the dark, often bloody tales associated with border history, Burgh Marsh stretches for several miles to the west of Carlisle. Stand at the spot where King Edward I died while waiting to take his army across the ford into Scotland, and the grassy flatlands seem to go on forever. Somewhere out there is the channel of the River Eden, inching its way ever closer to its rendezvous with Scotland's River Esk to flow together into the Solway Firth.

From the gate of St Michael's Church in **Burgh by Sands**, head west along the road for about 90m and then take the lane on the right – signposted Edward I Monument and Sandsfield.

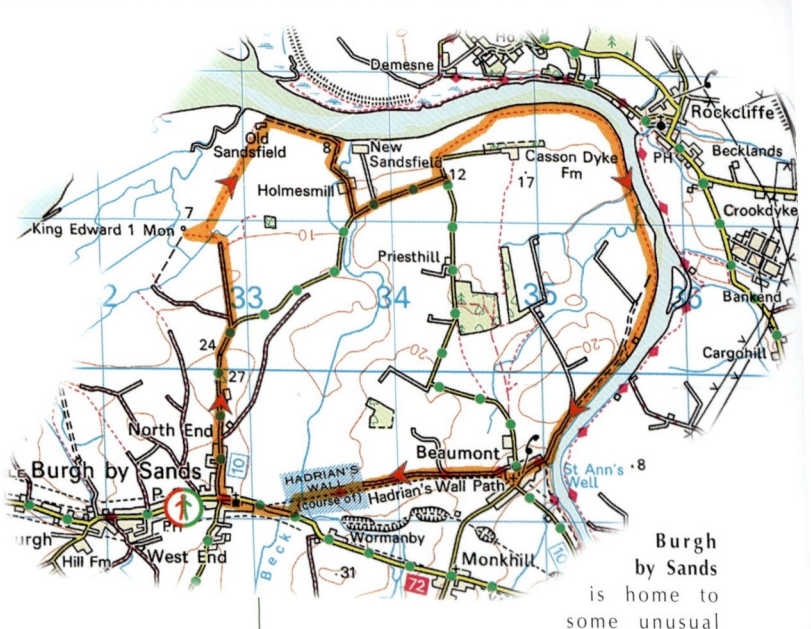

Burgh by Sands is home to some unusual architecture. There is a thatched cottage on the right, rare in Cumbria, as you head out of the village. Several clay dabbins can be found in the area. These are homes with walls built from a mixture of clay, stones and straw. It is a method of construction that probably dates back to the 15th century.

After about 1.3km, at a right-hand bend in the lane, turn left along a track, still following signs for the Edward I Monument. Bear right when it forks. Keeping straight on beyond a gate and stile, the track quickly peters out. After it does so, two stiles and a bridge, all in quick succession, lead on to the rough grazing at the edge of the marsh. Make your way to the fenced monument over to the left.

The **Edward I Monument** was built in 1685 to mark the site where the king died on 7 July 1307. Edward had been at war with the Scots since 1295, leading his army into battle on several occasions – hence his nickname 'Hammer of the Scots'. He died of

WALK 29 – BURGH MARSH

dysentery while camped here on the marsh, close to the place where his army was hoping to cross the River Eden at low tide to enter Scotland. His body was later taken to St Michael's Church in the village to lie in state before being taken back to London.

There is a bronze statue of Edward I on Burgh's village green close to the Greyhound Inn. It was unveiled by the Duke of Kent in 2007 to commemorate the 700th anniversary of Edward's death.

From the monument, head back towards the fence you crossed earlier, and then follow the line of this field boundary northeast across the access land until you reach **Old Sandsfield** and the **River Eden**. ▶

Go through the kissing-gate and follow the sign-posted route along the muddy embankment in front of the farmhouse. After about 450m of riverside walking, go through the gate on the right – signposted Burgh. Follow the lane away from the river, over a bridge and between the buildings at **Holmesmill**. Turn left at the T-junction and then left again when the lane bends right. As this too swings right, go through the kissing-gate to the left of the bend and bear right along the indistinct path to Beaumont. Watch for the two squat waymarker posts that

The monument is fenced to protect it from vandals

This old farmhouse was once an inn frequented by those trading with Scotland across the ford, or wath. It appears in Sir Walter Scott's *Red Gauntlet* as the inn called the Lady Lowther.

WALKING IN CUMBRIA'S EDEN VALLEY

Burgh Marsh

lead the way initially. Beyond these, keep to the left of the gorse to reach the first of two footbridges. After the second one, bear half-right to reach a stile at the river's edge. Once over this, head upstream on a faint grassy path that becomes increasingly overgrown.

As it flows into the Solway Firth, the **River Eden** plays host to one of the UK's few tidal bores. These occur when the leading edge of the incoming tide forms a wave as it is funnelled into a shallow narrowing river via a broad bay. In some conditions the tidal bore on the Eden reaches a height of about a metre and travels at seven knots. At these times the wave is clearly visible and the sudden rush of the water can be heard from quite some distance.

As you draw level with **Rockcliffe** on the opposite bank, the strip of land between the fence on the right and the Eden on the left narrows until you cross a stile and continue with the fence on your left. The path re-crosses the fence in a short while, but quickly crosses back again.

WALK 29 – BURGH MARSH

A pleasantly sleepy little village now, **Rockcliffe** has a colourful past. In the 18th century it was a commercial port and ship-building centre. Later it became an important staging post along the route used to smuggle whisky and brandy from Scotland to England. Due to differential duties on spirits, alcohol bought north of the border could be sold for five times as much in England. Several excise men were based in the village, but many Rockcliffe homes were storehouses for smuggled whisky.

After having crossed two bridges, bear right, away from the water's edge, for the next stile. Now continue parallel with the river and cross a steep-sided channel via a bridge. Immediately after crossing, turn right to continue parallel with the river again. As the hedgerow on the right draws close to the riverbank, you pick up a rough track. Follow this along the western edge of the access land. Beyond a gate, bear left along a surfaced lane and follow it into **Beaumont**.

Take the road on the right in front of the church – signposted Burgh via Sandsfield. After 100m, turn left along a narrow lane. You're now following the **Hadrian's**

HADRIAN'S WALL

Hadrian's Wall was constructed under the orders of the Emperor Hadrian after his visit to Britain in AD122. He wanted, according to his biographer, to 'separate the Romans from the barbarians'. Over the next six years professional soldiers, or legionaries, built a wall about 5m high and 80 Roman miles long (73 modern miles) from Wallsend on the River Tyne in the east to Bowness-on-Solway in Cumbria in the west. Today, it is a UNESCO World Heritage Site.

Little evidence remains of the wall west of Carlisle, although there are signs, as you leave the track and head towards Burgh on the Hadrian's Wall Path, of the Vallum – the high-sided defensive ditch the Romans built parallel to the wall. Watch for it after the sign requesting people to refrain from walking in single file. There would also have been a major fort at Burgh, known as Aballava, plus several marching camps around the Grinsdale and Beaumont area. The soldiers were based here to guard the waths.

WALKING IN CUMBRIA'S EDEN VALLEY

Looking down the Eden to Old Sandsfield

Wall Path, which runs for 84 miles from Wallsend on Tyneside to Bowness-on-Solway.

Do not be tempted by any turnings; simply keep straight ahead on this track. After narrowing and passing through a gate, the route keeps to the left of a line of trees where you are requested not to walk in single file to help protect the archaeology. Yellow waymarkers guide you across a gated bridge, beyond which you follow a fenced path to the road. Turn right and then, just after a layby, go through the kissing-gate to the right of the road to pick up the continuation of the Hadrian's Wall Path. Keep close to the hedge on your left and then, after the next gate, turn right along the road to return to St Michael's Church in **Burgh by Sands**.

WALK 30
Campfield Marsh and Bowness Common

Start/finish	Campfield Marsh RSPB reserve parking area at North Plain Farm (NY 198 615)
Distance	6¾ miles (11km)
Total ascent	58m (190ft)
Grade	1
Time	2¾hr
Terrain	Tracks; boardwalk across bog; farm paths; quiet roads
Maps	OS Explorer 314 or OS Landranger 85
Transport	Bowness-on-Solway is served by bus 93/93A
Facilities	Visitor information centre with toilets at reserve; Wallsend tearoom (summer only) and King's Arms in Bowness-on-Solway

Bowness Common, including the RSPB's Campfield Marsh site, forms part of the South Solway Mosses National Nature Reserve. This is one of the most important areas of lowland raised peat bog in England, and is home to a range of sphagnum mosses, sundew and other bog plants. Make sure you have your binoculars handy at all times. During the winter, teal, wigeon and other ducks can often be seen on the flooded fields, while huge flocks of barnacle and pink-footed geese feed on the salt-marsh. Visit in the spring and summer for impressive displays of wild flowers, to hear the curlews calling and to spot the colourful damselflies and dragonflies that are constantly flitting about across the moss.

From the car park, head back on to the main access track and turn left – away from the entrance to the reserve and following signs for Rogersceugh. The track eventually ends at a large wooden barrier, with the reserve's main hide to the left of it. Go through the first of the pedestrian gates on your right, still following signs for Rogersceugh.

Walking with the fence on your left across this field, you get a great view of Criffel on the other side of the

WALKING IN CUMBRIA'S EDEN VALLEY

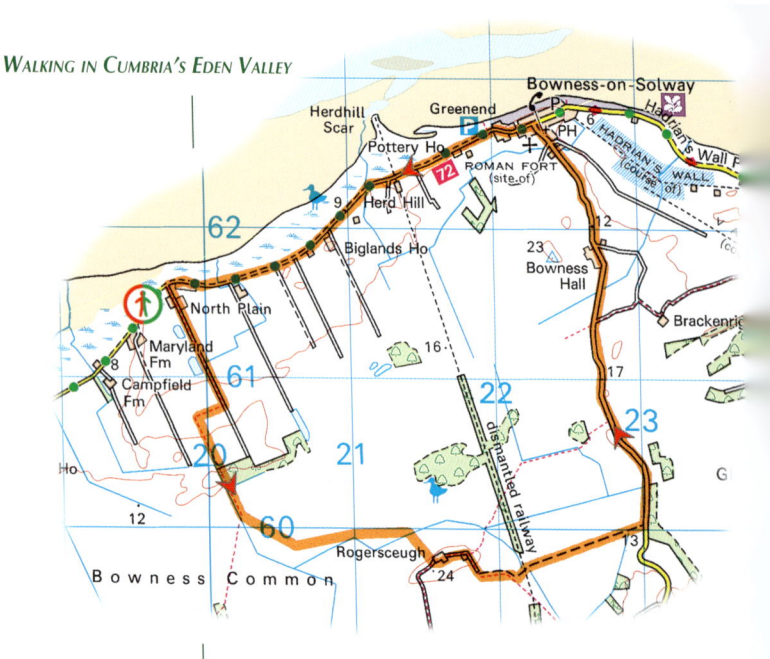

Winter on the Solway Firth

Solway Firth. When you reach a tiny pond, go through the gate on your left. Bear right along the grassy passage

Walk 30 – Campfield Marsh and Bowness Common

between the wet fields, quickly following it round to the left.

After the path has passed through a narrow area of woodland, you are able to look straight towards the Lake District fells. You soon encounter your first section of boardwalk, heading out across the wide, flat expanse of the peat bog. As a path peels off to Anthorn on the right, bear left – still signposted Rogersceugh. The farm buildings are directly ahead, perched on top of a tiny island of higher ground raised above the surrounding bog. This is a drumlin, deposited here by a glacier many thousands of years ago.

A clear but peaty path fills the short gap between sections of boardwalk. Where it resumes, there is a choice of two routes. Ignoring the boardwalk on the left, keep straight ahead, still making for the farm. When the boardwalk finally ends, follow the raised, grassy route round to the right. Go through a small gate and then cross the stile next to the large metal farm gate on the left. Keep straight ahead on the broad track to reach the abandoned farm at **Rogersceugh**.

The first building you come to contains information panels and a picnic bench. It is open to the elements on its north side, but provides shelter from passing showers.

Rogersceugh may be only 24m above sea level, but, because there's nothing higher than this for miles around, the views are tremendous. As well as the Scottish hills and the Lake District, the Pennines are also visible. The drumlin is also a great place to get a sense of the vastness of Bowness Common.

Continue on the track to the right of the farm buildings. Ignore two paths leading off as it follows a winding route away from Rogersceugh. It ends just before a pair of large farm gates with a smaller pedestrian gate between them. Go through the latter to access a grassy track running beside a drainage ditch. In about 800m, this track leads on to a minor road opposite an entrance to the reserve at **Glasson Moss**. Turn left and follow the road

Bowness-on-Solway marks the western end of Hadrian's Wall, built in AD122 to defend this remote frontier of the Roman Empire from the Pictish people to the north.

to **Bowness-on-Solway**, passing **Bowness Hall** along the way. ◄

On reaching the T-junction in the village, turn left again – signposted Anthorn and Cardurnock. (The King's Arms pub is on the right at this junction.) The entrance to the Campfield Marsh reserve, where the walk started, is on the left, almost 3km from this junction.

As you head out along the marsh road, you'll see a spit of land sticking out into the estuary. This is **Herdhill Scar** and it holds the remains of the southern end of the viaduct that once crossed the channel here. Built in 1868 and nearly 2km long, it was, at the time, one of Europe's longest railway viaducts.

> The **viaduct** was closed to traffic in 1921, but, before it was demolished in 1934, it was often used by pedestrians crossing from Scotland to England to take advantage of the more relaxed Sunday licensing laws south of the border. There are stories of drinkers, heading back into Scotland at the end of an evening's drinking, falling off the viaduct and drowning in the water below.

Salt-marshes

WALK 30 – CAMPFIELD MARSH AND BOWNESS COMMON

If you tire of the road, you could take to the marsh itself, but watch carefully for the deep pools and channels that exist between the road and the water's edge. As well as the damp ground, thick stands of gorse also make it difficult to get on and off the marsh in places.

SALMON IN THE RIVER EDEN

The River Eden used to be one of the most important salmon fisheries in the country. In fact, many of the largest salmon ever caught in England were caught in these waters. Henry I granted part of the fishery to the city of Carlisle in the 12th century.

In December and January Atlantic salmon swim from the sea to the higher reaches of the Eden, sometimes as far upstream as Stenkrith at Kirkby Stephen, to spawn. The female lays her eggs on the bottom of shallow rivers and streams, covering them with gravel after they have been fertilised by the male. The young hatch in April and May, and spend the first six years of their lives in the river. They eventually migrate to the sea and remain there for up to three years, returning to spawn in the area of the river in which they were born.

Although stocks have declined, due to a combination of over-fishing at sea and pollution, the Eden is still a fine salmon river and remains one of the cleanest in England.

One of the more unusual methods used to catch both salmon and trout is known as haaf-netting. This ancient method of fishing is said to date back to the Norsemen and is still practised where the river enters the Solway Firth. Only a small but hardy and determined group of fishermen – there are about 50 left in Cumbria – continue to use the 'haaf net' (meaning 'sea net'). Like a giant butterfly net, it is mounted on a frame about 6m wide and 1.5m high and supported by three legs. The fishermen heave these cumbersome contraptions on to their shoulders, tramp out over the gloopy mudflats and stand waist-deep in the cold water waiting for the fish to come along. They hold the central 'leg' as the net is placed across the current. The net then streams out in the water and, when fish swim into it, the other two legs of the frame are allowed to float to the surface. This traps the fish, which are then dispatched by a blow from a mallet, known as a 'nep'.

WALKING IN CUMBRIA'S EDEN VALLEY

APPENDIX A
Route summary table

Walk no	Start	Finish	Distance	Time	Grade	Page
1	Garsdale station	Kirkby Stephen station	12¼ miles (19.5km)	7hr	5	28
2	Thrang Beck	Thrang Beck	10¼ miles (16.5km)	5¾hr	4	34
3	Layby on B6270	Layby on B6270	7 miles (11.5km)	3¾hr	3	39
4	Ravenstonedale	Ravenstonedale	7¾ miles (12.5km)	3½hr	2–3	44
5	Smardale	Smardale	7 miles (11.5km)	3¾hr	2–3	48
6	Kirkby Stephen	Kirkby Stephen	9 miles (14.5km)	4½hr	2	53
7	Kirkby Stephen station	Appleby station	15 miles (24km)	6½hr	3	59
8	Orton	Orton	8¾ miles (14km)	4½hr	2–3	67
9	Near Sunbiggin	Near Sunbiggin	11 miles (18km)	5hr	2–3	72
10	Crosby Ravensworth	Crosby Ravensworth	6½ miles (10.5km)	3½hr	2–3	78
11	Bampton	Bampton	5¼ miles (8.5km)	2½ hr	2	83
12	King's Meaburn	King's Meaburn	6¼ miles (10km)	3hr	2	88
13	Appleby	Appleby	7 miles (11.5km)	3¼hr	1–2	92
14	Murton	Murton	13¾ miles (22km)	8hr	5	97
15	Murton	Murton	4 miles (6.5km)	2¾hr	2–3	104

APPENDIX A – ROUTE SUMMARY TABLE

Walk no	Start	Finish	Distance	Time	Grade	Page
16	Dufton	Dufton	6 miles (9.5km)	3hr	1–2	107
17	Dufton	Dufton	4 miles (6.5km)	2¾hr	2–3	112
18	Dufton	Dufton	10 miles (16km)	5½hr	4	116
19	Blencarn	Blencarn	10¼ miles (16.5km)	5¾hr	4	120
20	Little Salkeld	Little Salkeld	4¾ miles (7.5km)	2hr	1	125
21	Melmerby	Melmerby	11 miles (18km)	5¾hr	4	129
22	Kirkoswald	Kirkoswald	6¼ miles (10km)	2¾hr	1	134
23	Armathwaite	Armathwaite	3½ miles (5.5km)	1½hr	1	139
24	Croglin	Croglin	5 miles (8.2km)	2¾hr	2	142
25	Wetheral	Wetheral	4½ miles (7km)	2hr	1	146
26	Talkin	Talkin	6¼ miles (10km)	3¾hr	2–3	151
27	Talkin Tarn	Talkin Tarn	7¾ miles (12.5km)	4½hr	2	155
28	Lanercost Bridge	Lanercost Bridge	4 miles (6.5km)	2hr	1–2	161
29	Burgh by Sands	Burgh by Sands	7 miles (11.5km)	3hr	1–2	165
30	Campfield Marsh	Campfield Marsh	6¾ miles (11km)	2¾hr	1	171

APPENDIX B
Useful contacts

Tourist Information Centres

Kirkby Stephen
Market Place
Kirkby Stephen
CA17 4QN
tel 017683 71199
www.visiteden.co.uk

Appleby
Moot Hall
Boroughgate
Appleby
CA16 6YV
tel 017683 51177
www.visiteden.co.uk

Penrith
Middlegate
Penrith
CA11 7PT
tel 01768 867466
www.visiteden.co.uk

Carlisle
Old Town Hall
Green Market
Carlisle
CA3 8JH
tel 01228 598 596
Email: tourism@carlisle.gov.uk

Brampton
Moot Hall
Market Place
Brampton
CA8 1RW
tel 016977 3433

Other useful sources of information
Access restrictions
www.openaccess.naturalengland.org.uk

Traveline
tel 0871 200 2233
www.traveline.info

Settle–Carlisle Railway
www.settle-carlisle.co.uk

Mountain Weather Information Service
www.mwis.org.uk

Lanercost Priory
tel 01697 73030
www.english-heritage.org.uk

Cumbria Wildlife Trust
tel 01539 816300
www.cumbriawildlifetrust.org.uk

Eden Rivers Trust
tel 01768 866788
www.edenriverstrust.org.uk

DOWNLOAD THE ROUTES IN GPX FORMAT

All the routes in this guide are available for download from:

www.cicerone.co.uk/901/GPX

as GPX files. You should be able to load them into most formats of mobile device, whether GPS or smartphone.

When you go to this link, you will be asked for your email address and where you purchased the guide, and have the option to subscribe to the Cicerone e-newsletter.

CICERONE
www.cicerone.co.uk

NOTES

LISTING OF CICERONE GUIDES

BRITISH ISLES CHALLENGES, COLLECTIONS AND ACTIVITIES

The Big Rounds
The Book of the Bivvy
The Book of the Bothy
The C2C Cycle Route
The Mountains of England and Wales:
Vol 1 Wales
Vol 2 England
The National Trails
Walking The End to End Trail
Cycling Land's End to John o' Groats

SCOTLAND

Ben Nevis and Glen Coe
Cycle Touring in Northern Scotland
Cycling in the Hebrides
Great Mountain Days in Scotland
Mountain Biking in Southern and Central Scotland
Mountain Biking in West and North West Scotland
Not the West Highland Way Scotland
Scotland's Best Small Mountains
Scotland's Mountain Ridges
Skye's Cuillin Ridge Traverse
The Borders Abbeys Way
The Great Glen Way
The Great Glen Way Map Booklet
The Hebridean Way
The Hebrides
The Isle of Mull
The Isle of Skye
The Skye Trail
The Southern Upland Way
The Speyside Way
The Speyside Way Map Booklet
The West Highland Way
The West Highland Way Map Booklet
Walking Ben Lawers, Rannoch and Atholl
Walking in the Cairngorms
Walking in the Pentland Hills
Walking in the Scottish Borders
Walking in the Southern Uplands
Walking in Torridon
Walking Loch Lomond and the Trossachs
Walking on Arran
Walking on Harris and Lewis
Walking on Jura, Islay and Colonsay
Walking on Rum and the Small Isles
Walking on the Orkney and Shetland Isles
Walking on Uist and Barra
Walking the Cape Wrath Trail

Walking the Corbetts
Vol 1 South of the Great Glen
Vol 2 North of the Great Glen
Walking the Galloway Hills
Walking the Munros
Vol 1 – Southern, Central and Western Highlands
Vol 2 – Northern Highlands and the Cairngorms
Winter Climbs Ben Nevis and Glen Coe
Winter Climbs in the Cairngorms

NORTHERN ENGLAND TRAILS

Hadrian's Wall Path
Hadrian's Wall Path Map Booklet
The Coast to Coast Walk
The Coast to Coast Walk Map Booklet
The Pennine Way
The Pennine Way Map Booklet
Walking the Dales Way
Walking the Dales Way Map Booklet
Walking the Tour of the Lake District

NORTH EAST ENGLAND, YORKSHIRE DALES AND PENNINES

Cycling in the Yorkshire Dales
Great Mountain Days in the Pennines
Mountain Biking in the Yorkshire Dales
St Oswald's Way and St Cuthbert's Way
The Cleveland Way and the Yorkshire Wolds Way
The Cleveland Way Map Booklet
The North York Moors
The Reivers Way
The Teesdale Way
Trail and Fell Running in the Yorkshire Dales
Walking in County Durham
Walking in Northumberland
Walking in the North Pennines
Walking in the Yorkshire Dales: North and East
Walking in the Yorkshire Dales: South and West

NORTH WEST ENGLAND AND THE ISLE OF MAN

Cycling the Pennine Bridleway
Cycling the Reivers Route
Cycling the Way of the Roses
Hadrian's Cycleway
Isle of Man Coastal Path
The Lancashire Cycleway
The Lune Valley and Howgills
Walking in Cumbria's Eden Valley
Walking in Lancashire

Walking in the Forest of Bowland and Pendle
Walking on the Isle of Man
Walking on the West Pennine Moors
Walks in Silverdale and Arnside

LAKE DISTRICT

Cycling in the Lake District
Great Mountain Days in the Lake District
Joss Naylor's Lakes, Meres and Waters of the Lake District
Lake District Winter Climbs
Lake District: High Level and Fell Walks
Lake District: Low Level and Lake Walks
Mountain Biking in the Lake District
Outdoor Adventures with Children – Lake District
Scrambles in the Lake District – North
Scrambles in the Lake District – South
The Cumbria Way
Trail and Fell Running in the Lake District
Walking the Lake District Fells:
Borrowdale
Buttermere
Coniston
Keswick
Langdale
Mardale and the Far East
Patterdale
Wasdale

DERBYSHIRE, PEAK DISTRICT AND MIDLANDS

Cycling in the Peak District
Dark Peak Walks
Scrambles in the Dark Peak
Walking in Derbyshire
Walking in the Peak District – White Peak East
Walking in the Peak District – White Peak West

SOUTHERN ENGLAND

20 Classic Sportive Rides in South East England
20 Classic Sportive Rides in South West England
Cycling in the Cotswolds
Mountain Biking on the North Downs
Mountain Biking on the South Downs
Suffolk Coast and Heath Walks
The Cotswold Way
The Cotswold Way Map Booklet
The Great Stones Way
The Kennet and Avon Canal
The Lea Valley Walk

The North Downs Way
The North Downs Way Map Booklet
The Peddars Way and Norfolk Coast path
The Pilgrims' Way
The Ridgeway National Trail
The Ridgeway National Trail Map Booklet
The South Downs Way
The South Downs Way Map Booklet
The Thames Path
The Thames Path Map Booklet
The Two Moors Way
The Two Moors Way Map Booklet
Walking Hampshire's Test Way
Walking in Cornwall
Walking in Essex
Walking in Kent
Walking in London
Walking in Norfolk
Walking in the Chilterns
Walking in the Cotswolds
Walking in the Isles of Scilly
Walking in the New Forest
Walking in the North Wessex Downs
Walking on Dartmoor
Walking on Guernsey
Walking on Jersey
Walking on the Isle of Wight
Walking the Jurassic Coast
Walking the South West Coast Path
Walking the South West Coast Path Map Booklets:
  Vol 1: Minehead to St Ives
  Vol 2: St Ives to Plymouth
  Vol 3: Plymouth to Poole
Walks in the South Downs National Park

WALES AND WELSH BORDERS

Cycle Touring in Wales
Cycling Lon Las Cymru
Glyndwr's Way
Great Mountain Days in Snowdonia
Hillwalking in Shropshire
Hillwalking in Wales – Vols 1&2
Mountain Walking in Snowdonia
Offa's Dyke Path
Offa's Dyke Path Map Booklet
Ridges of Snowdonia
Scrambles in Snowdonia
Snowdonia: 30 Low-level and easy walks – North
Snowdonia: 30 Low-level and easy walks – South
The Cambrian Way
The Ceredigion and Snowdonia Coast Paths
The Pembrokeshire Coast Path
Pembrokeshire Coast Path Map Booklet
The Severn Way

The Snowdonia Way
The Wales Coast Path
The Wye Valley Walk
Walking in Carmarthenshire
Walking in Pembrokeshire
Walking in the Forest of Dean
Walking in the Wye Valley
Walking on Gower
Walking on the Brecon Beacons
Walking the Shropshire Way

INTERNATIONAL CHALLENGES, COLLECTIONS AND ACTIVITIES

Canyoning in the Alps
Europe's High Points

AFRICA

Kilimanjaro
The High Atlas
Walks and Scrambles in the Moroccan Anti-Atlas
Walking in the Drakensberg

ALPS CROSS-BORDER ROUTES

100 Hut Walks in the Alps
Alpine Ski Mountaineering
  Vol 1 – Western Alps
  Vol 2 – Central and Eastern Alps
Chamonix to Zermatt
The Karnischer Hohenweg
The Tour of the Bernina
Tour of Monte Rosa
Tour of the Matterhorn
Trail Running – Chamonix and the Mont Blanc region
Trekking in the Alps
Trekking in the Silvretta and Ratikon Alps
Trekking Munich to Venice
Trekking the Tour of Mont Blanc
Walking in the Alps

PYRENEES AND FRANCE/SPAIN CROSS-BORDER ROUTES

Shorter Treks in the Pyrenees
The GR10 Trail
The GR11 Trail
The Pyrenean Haute Route
The Pyrenees
Walks and Climbs in the Pyrenees

AUSTRIA

Innsbruck Mountain Adventures
The Adlerweg
Trekking in Austria's Hohe Tauern
Trekking in the Stubai Alps
Trekking in the Zillertal Alps
Walking in Austria
Walking in the Salzkammergut: the Austrian Lake District

EASTERN EUROPE

The Danube Cycleway Vol 2
The High Tatras
The Mountains of Romania
Walking in Bulgaria's National Parks

Walking in Hungary

FRANCE, BELGIUM AND LUXEMBOURG

Chamonix Mountain Adventures
Cycle Touring in France
Cycling London to Paris
Cycling the Canal de la Garonne
Cycling the Canal du Midi
Mont Blanc Walks
Mountain Adventures in the Maurienne
Short Treks on Corsica
The GR20 Corsica
The GR5 Trail
The GR5 Trail – Benelux and Lorraine
The GR5 Trail – Vosges and Jura
The Grand Traverse of the Massif Central
The Loire Cycle Route
The Moselle Cycle Route
The River Rhone Cycle Route
The Way of St James – Le Puy to the Pyrenees
Tour of the Queyras
Trekking in the Vanoise
Trekking the Cathar Way
Trekking the Robert Louis Stevenson Trail
Vanoise Ski Touring
Via Ferratas of the French Alps
Walking in Provence – East
Walking in Provence – West
Walking in the Ardennes
Walking in the Auvergne
Walking in the Briançonnais
Walking in the Dordogne
Walking in the Haute Savoie: North
Walking in the Haute Savoie: South
Walking on Corsica

GERMANY

Hiking and Cycling in the Black Forest
The Danube Cycleway Vol 1
The Rhine Cycle Route
The Westweg
Walking in the Bavarian Alps

IRELAND

The Wild Atlantic Way and Western Ireland
Walking the Wicklow Way

ITALY

Italy's Sibillini National Park
Shorter Walks in the Dolomites
Ski Touring and Snowshoeing in the Dolomites
The Way of St Francis
Trekking in the Apennines
Trekking in the Dolomites

Trekking the Giants' Trail: Alta Via 1 through the Italian Pennine Alps
Via Ferratas of the Italian Dolomites Vols 1&2
Walking and Trekking in the Gran Paradiso
Walking in Abruzzo
Walking in Italy's Cinque Terre
Walking in Italy's Stelvio National Park
Walking in Sicily
Walking in the Dolomites
Walking in Tuscany
Walking in Umbria
Walking Lake Como and Maggiore
Walking Lake Garda and Iseo
Walking on the Amalfi Coast
Walking the Via Francigena pilgrim route – Parts 2&3
Walks and Treks in the Maritime Alps

MEDITERRANEAN

The High Mountains of Crete
Trekking in Greece
Treks and Climbs in Wadi Rum, Jordan
Walking and Trekking in Zagori
Walking and Trekking on Corfu
Walking in Cyprus
Walking on Malta
Walking on the Greek Islands – the Cyclades

NEW ZEALAND & AUSTRALIA

Hiking the Overland Track

NORTH AMERICA

The John Muir Trail
The Pacific Crest Trail

SOUTH AMERICA

Aconcagua and the Southern Andes
Hiking and Biking Peru's Inca Trails
Torres del Paine

SCANDINAVIA, ICELAND AND GREENLAND

Hiking in Norway – South
Trekking in Greenland – The Arctic Circle Trail
Trekking the Kungsleden
Walking and Trekking in Iceland

SLOVENIA, CROATIA, SERBIA, MONTENEGRO AND ALBANIA

Mountain Biking in Slovenia
The Islands of Croatia
The Julian Alps of Slovenia
The Mountains of Montenegro
The Peaks of the Balkans Trail
The Slovene Mountain Trail
Walking in Slovenia: The Karavanke
Walks and Treks in Croatia

SPAIN AND PORTUGAL

Camino de Santiago: Camino Frances
Coastal Walks in Andalucia
Cycling the Camino de Santiago
Mountain Walking in Mallorca
Mountain Walking in Southern Catalunya
Portugal's Rota Vicentina
Spain's Sendero Historico: The GR1
The Andalucian Coast to Coast Walk
The Camino del Norte and Camino Primitivo
The Camino Ingles and Ruta do Mar
The Camino Portugues
The Mountains of Nerja
The Mountains of Ronda and Grazalema
The Sierras of Extremadura
Trekking in Mallorca
Trekking in the Canary Islands
Trekking the GR7 in Andalucia
Walking and Trekking in the Sierra Nevada
Walking in Andalucia
Walking in Menorca
Walking in Portugal
Walking in the Algarve
Walking in the Cordillera Cantabrica
Walking on Gran Canaria
Walking on La Gomera and El Hierro
Walking on La Palma
Walking on Lanzarote and Fuerteventura
Walking on Madeira
Walking on Tenerife
Walking on the Azores
Walking on the Costa Blanca
Walking the Camino dos Faros

SWITZERLAND

Switzerland's Jura Crest Trail
The Swiss Alpine Pass Route – Via Alpina Route 1
The Swiss Alps
Tour of the Jungfrau Region
Walking in the Bernese Oberland
Walking in the Engadine – Switzerland
Walking in the Valais
Walking in Zermatt and Saas-Fee

JAPAN AND ASIA

Hiking and Trekking in the Japan Alps and Mount Fuji
Japan's Kumano Kodo Pilgrimage
Trekking in Tajikistan

HIMALAYA

Annapurna
Everest: A Trekker's Guide
Trekking in Bhutan
Trekking in Ladakh
Trekking in the Himalaya

MOUNTAIN LITERATURE

8000 metres
A Walk in the Clouds
Abode of the Gods
Fifty Years of Adventure
The Pennine Way – the Path, the People, the Journey
Unjustifiable Risk?

TECHNIQUES

Fastpacking
Geocaching in the UK
Map and Compass
Outdoor Photography
Polar Exploration
The Mountain Hut Book

MINI GUIDES

Alpine Flowers
Navigation
Pocket First Aid and Wilderness Medicine
Snow

For full information on all our guides, books and eBooks, visit our website:
www.cicerone.co.uk

CICERONE

Trust Cicerone to guide your next adventure, wherever it may be around the world...

Discover guides for hiking, mountain walking, backpacking, trekking, trail running, cycling and mountain biking, ski touring, climbing and scrambling in Britain, Europe and worldwide.

Connect with Cicerone online and find inspiration.

- buy books and ebooks
- articles, advice and trip reports
- podcasts and live events
- GPX files and updates
- regular newsletter

cicerone.co.uk